CALLED TO ACT

CALLED TO ACT

The Origins of Christian Responsibility

MICHAEL W. HOPKINS

CHURCH
PUBLISHING
INCORPORATED

Church Publishing
19 East 34th Street
New York, NY 10016

Cover art: carstenbrandt / istockphoto.com / stock photo ID: 1413807614
Cover design by Nord Compo

Library of Congress Cataloging-in-Publication Data

Names: Hopkins, Michael W., author.
Title: Called to act : the origins of Christian responsibility / Michael W. Hopkins.
Description: New York, NY : Church Publishing, 2023. | Includes bibliographical references.
Identifiers: LCCN 2023012745 (print) | LCCN 2023012746 (ebook) | ISBN 9781640656505 (paperback) | ISBN 9781640656512 (ebook)
Subjects: LCSH: Christian life. | Sacraments—Christianity. | Sacraments—Catholic Church. | Baptism.
Classification: LCC BV4501.3 .H6754 2023 (print) | LCC BV4501.3 (ebook) | DDC 248.4—dc23/eng/20230621
LC record available at https://lccn.loc.gov/2023012745
LC ebook record available at https://lccn.loc.gov/2023012746

Little children, let us love, not in word or speech,
but in truth and action.
1 John 3:18

Dedicated to the memory of Dr. Verna Dozier &
The Rev. Dr. Louis Weil
Teachers, Mentors, Friends

Contents

Foreword

Though we have never served in the same Episcopal diocese, I have known Michael Hopkins for a good portion of my ordained life. Over the years we have seen one another praying in the chapel stalls of the Monastery of St. John the Evangelist in Massachusetts and working the floor of General Convention to get a resolution passed. We have served like-minded diverse congregations in neighboring dioceses, and I've been an ally and advocate in his work for the full inclusion of LGBTQIA peoples in the church.

If you didn't know Michael, you could read his résumé, or see the fruits of his ministry with Integrity, an advocacy group working for the full inclusion of LGBTQIA peoples in the life and ministry of the Episcopal Church, and assume him to be primarily politically motivated. That would be to misunderstand him and his grounding in a theology of baptism, one that has implications for how Christians are to live in the world. Over the course of this book, the notion of baptism as integral to action in the world is driven home in stories drawn from the early church, contemporary religious and political movements, and compellingly, Michael's life.

With rich and lively narrative, Michael weaves images and stories from ancient religious texts (both within and outside the scriptural canon) together with examples born from the rich farming communities of Upstate New York that birthed some of the most memorable religious movements of the eighteenth and nineteenth centuries. From the introduction on, it is evident how these contexts have formed his life and pastoral ministry lived out largely in times of radical societal and political change.

My own baptism in the spring of 1989 bore little resemblance to the baptism of Priscilla and Julius described in the early pages of this book. Though I had longed to be baptized since I was a child, it wouldn't be until I was twenty-two years old that I would finally find a community within which to make this life-altering commitment. Far from a risky and secretive event, my baptism was a socially acceptable, if not expected, rite of passage performed at one of the most prominent Episcopal churches in the world. Performed on the feast of Pentecost at 11:15 a.m. at Trinity Church Wall Street, about the only things my baptism had in common with the baptisms given to those new members of the early church were water, oil, candles, mystery, a bishop, and most importantly, the sense that the values, choices, and framework that shaped my life was reoriented and changed forever.

Indeed, I would go on to serve as a priest for nearly twenty years and now as bishop for six. Over the course of more than twenty-five years in ordained ministry in the Episcopal Church I have baptized dozens of infants and adults alike. Each and every time, I did so with the firm belief that this assent to living in a Godward direction in community with others is a life-altering event for the individual as well as the faith community that witnesses to the baptism. In the hyper-individualized American culture that we live in, to be baptized into the Christian faith in which we choose to "live no longer for ourselves alone" continues to be a most radical act with the power to transform the world.

In *Called to Act: The Origins of Christian Responsibility*, Michael has given us a text to be read and reflected upon by adult converts preparing for baptism, parents bringing their young children to the baptismal font, and anyone seeking to better understand how they fit within this larger story of Christian belonging and living. Through encounters with scripture, strangers, and parishioners, Michael wrestles with baptism as a singular act with lifelong implications. In short, he helps others sort out how to live: day by day, issue by issue. With the seemingly intractable challenges the world is facing, we need the transformational power of Christians acting out of care for the other, the stranger, and the common good. As it has been for me, I hope that you will find in these pages inspiration, encouragement, and strength for the journey.

The Rt. Rev. Jennifer Baskerville-Burrows
Bishop of the Episcopal Diocese of Indianapolis
Indianapolis, Indiana
May 2023

Introduction

Instead of relation between the weak and the strong, there is merely a relationship between human beings. The awareness of this fact marks the supreme moment of human dignity.
—Howard Thurman, *Jesus and the Disinherited*

G od has created all human beings equal in rights, duties and dignity, and has called them to live together as brothers and sisters." This vision for life together was part of a joint statement from Pope Francis and the Grand Imam Ahmad Al-Tayyeb in February 2019 after their meeting in Abu Dhabi. It inspired Francis's encyclical *Fratelli tutti* (literally "all the brothers"), issued a little more than a year later. It is a simple vision that raises many questions about the responsibility of all people, including Christians, for their day-to-day living in the world.

No one can reasonably deny Francis's observation in *Fratelli tutti* that the world is teetering on disaster on many fronts. Perhaps this has always been true, but an urgent situation exists today, one that has been exacerbated by political, economic, and social divisions, an environmental crisis that is no longer a threat but a grim reality, and a lifestyle of prejudice and violence growing globally.

Christians living in this world have three choices: They can rest their faith on a hope of heaven and leave the world and its ugliness behind; they can join in the division, claiming their exclusive hold on what is right and wrong, playing out their version of the judgment of God on the world; or they can take responsibility for their part in the world, seeking the common good and following Jesus's call to "love one another as I have loved you."

To put the question of this book succinctly, "What is a Christian's responsibility in her or his daily living?" The question is deceptively simple. We could answer with Jesus's command to love. That is not, however, adequate. To answer the question, we have to dive deep into the many aspects of daily life about which many Christians are uneasy or bewildered. Among these are questions of economic, political, and cultural life.

For example, Pope Francis asked the question, "Can our world function without politics?"[1] It was meant as a rhetorical question. The answer is clearly "no." Yet many of us wish the answer were "yes." Politics may be necessary, but it is also clearly part of the problem. In our day, as in many times throughout history (including United States history), politics does not bring people together to problem-solve. "Bipartisanship" is rare. Politics seems to cause more division and stalemate than positive outcomes.

* * *

What does faith have to do with politics or economics or any of the daily decisions we have to make? This has been a sore question throughout history. Mixing religion and politics (including economic and cultural issues) has gotten innumerable pastors into trouble, not to mention entire congregations. Some version of "I don't want to hear politics from the pulpit" has been heard by a significant majority of both ordained and lay leaders of churches. In the United States, the constitutional separation of church and state is frequently held up as the basis of such an argument. Yet what the Constitution truly says is, "Congress shall make no law respecting an establishment of religion, or prohibiting the free exercise thereof." Surely the "free exercise of religion" includes one's religious faith affecting one's political stances. And while it is true that churches and other religious institutions are prohibited from certain political acts as a condition of keeping their tax-exempt status, this is not (as perhaps many misunderstand) a blanket separation of religion and politics. In fact, it only applies to the endorsing of candidates or parties in elections.

Still, there is much confusion. I write as one who shares in the confusion and longs for some clarity. My longing is increasingly urgent, mostly because the rise of so-called Christian nationalism so blurs the lines between faith and social policy that many people of faith want their religious leaders not to have anything to do with politics. I agree—if the goal is the politicization of faith or the church, the political weaponizing of Jesus, or, on the other hand, the turning of political ideology into religious dogma.

* * *

My purpose is to ask questions about Christian responsibility, beginning with the primary sacrament of the church—Holy Baptism. The rite of baptism is about "origins." It is the sacramental beginning of our Christian life. It raises the basic question: Are there implications for our daily life in baptism, that most fundamental of Christian rites? To be up front and honest, that is a rhetorical question for me. My answer is "yes." However, there is more to the answer than simply "yes" or "no." What are those implications, and how might our understanding and experience of baptism direct our fundamental outlook on the world around us, especially for our call to action in that world?

Baptism is also my chosen framework because it is the primary sacrament of Christian responsibility. There are a myriad of moments in the practice of our faith that call for Christians to act out this work, from the biblical imperative of covenant, to the church's primary act of unity, the Eucharist, to our pledge to follow Jesus in the ways of peace and justice, and to that most central of causes, the dignity of every human being.

It is important that I make my biases clear. I am a member of The Episcopal Church and a priest. I served parishes for twenty-three years before my retirement and have continued to serve as best I can. Those parishes have been in suburban, urban, and rural settings. My engagement in politics and economic and social policy is as an ordinary citizen. I am a registered Democrat, although I live in a majority Republican part of the country, that of the Southern Tier of Upstate New York. I do not much care for the labels of conservative, moderate, or liberal, although, admittedly, most of the time I lean toward the latter. I will say, however, that it is not my intention to persuade anyone as to where they should stand in relation to party or labels. My purpose is to assist you in a critical engagement with your public and social life, wherever you stand. I do not believe that Christians have the option of eschewing public life. I believe we must be engaged, and always critically so.

In speaking of baptism, I will be using the rite from the current edition of the Book of Common Prayer. I trust that my exploration will be helpful to someone from any Christian tradition, especially sacramental ones. It is my aim to be in dialogue with many voices—Anglican/Episcopalian and those from other traditions. In doing so I am looking for ways of understanding the church's relationship to public policy and public life that have held up over time and served a broad spectrum of people. As to gendered language, I have not altered any quotes in regard to masculine language for God or humankind. I will let these quotes stand as they are, knowing, in almost every case, the more inclusive sense of "man" or "men" is intended.

I have used the term "the Way" in most of my chapter titles, a term that has biblical roots. After witnessing the stoning of the deacon Stephen for blasphemy, Saul (later to become Paul) went to the high priest and asked for written evidence of his authority so that he could go to Damascus, an early center of Christian activity, and "if he found any who belonged to the Way, men or women, he might bring them bound to Jerusalem" (Acts 9:2). The use of the description crops up several times in the Acts of the Apostles. I believe this designation of the followers of Jesus is instructive in that it clearly denotes a way of life and not a doctrinal belief.

As to my method, I believe theology needs a narrative structure. If we are "people of the Book" we are also "people of the Story." So, I begin my exploration with my own baptismal story in chapter 1 and then reach back into the church's ancient past for the story in chapter 2. Each of the subsequent chapters will contain some measure of story, most of them (but not all) from my own experience. I do not rely on my own story because I consider it to be at all exceptional. It is not, although it has its moments of particularity. This is true not only of my story, but yours as well. I hope in this way to engage your own story. Again, I believe this attentiveness to story is the jumping off point of all good and helpful theological reflection.

Finally, I must say that I know myself to be a person who lives with great privilege. As a gay man I have had my share of struggles both in the church and in the world, struggles that many times have brought me to the brink of despair. I have not, however, had to live in the crush of poverty, racism, and sexism. I have tried all my adult life to try to hear the voices of those without such privilege on their own terms, although I have not always succeeded. I write this book with the conviction that we must reach across the many barriers put up between us, both those of our own making and those that have been imposed upon us, and we must learn to act together, as surely as we are called to be responsible together for the gift of life.

CHAPTER 1

The Indissoluble Bond

The implications of Baptism are not narrowly religious in their content. Baptism has serious ethical implications which involve us in the fostering of God's will in all the dimensions of human life.
—Louis Weil,
Sacrament & Liturgy: The Outward Signs

I do not remember my baptism, even though I was just shy of five years old. While preparing for ordination in 1984, I had to search for proof the sacrament had happened; my only clue was the church where it had taken place. No one else in the family seemed sure of anything but that, yes, there had been a baptism, and, yes, it had happened in the Wallace Methodist Church. I had to ask for a certified letter from the then-current pastor. Some twenty-five years later, I found the original certificate in a shoebox of stuff that my mother had found in one of her closet-cleaning sessions.

My baptism was on Palm Sunday, April 3, 1966, in a little country Methodist church, the church of my Hopkins ancestors in the hamlet of Wallace, New York, on the western edge of the Finger Lakes. My sister Leann, a little over a year old, was baptized with me. The church is long closed. Someone tried to turn it into a community hall and bed and breakfast, which did not pan out. My husband and I came very close to buying it in 2015. We were moving south from Rochester to the Southern Tier of New York (the counties on the border with Pennsylvania between Binghamton and Jamestown). We looked at the church not only as a place to live, since the parish house had been turned into a home, but also as a potential place for ministry. One of our thoughts was to run it as a small retreat house for ordained people and their families. When our loan application got flagged as a business loan because of our plans, with additional terms we could not meet, we had to pull out.

Walking inside the church during those initial considerations, I was taken aback by the emptiness—all the furniture was gone: pulpit, communion table, baptismal font, organ, pews. It looked exposed to me, even violated, like someone was trying to dissipate the holiness of prayers said over the course of a hundred years. The stained-glass windows remained, most likely because they did not contain any directly Christian themes. They added warm color to the room. There was still a stained-glass five-pointed star above where the pulpit and communion table had been, so we were going to name the place "Epiphany House," to honor the day the church celebrates the magi's following of a star to Bethlehem. There was one memorial plaque left on the wall, stating that the lighting had been given by my great-grandfather, Fred Hopkins, in 1952.

Our attempt to buy the church property was not the best idea that we ever had, but the emotional attachment for me was very strong. I sought connection to an ancestry, physical and spiritual. It was romantic and sentimental, of course, but I longed to keep the place alive with the memories that belonged to it, and to me, faint as they were. I had a strong sense that a portion of the mystery of my life lived in those walls. There were memories there of things done, perhaps for mundane reasons—silent memories, yet holy.

I remember nothing about attending church in those early days, although in the same shoebox as my baptismal certificate was another one: a Sunday school certificate from when I was in kindergarten. My mother tells me I walked to Sunday school (until I was four and a half we lived only a quarter of a mile from the church), although this does not entirely make sense to me, because there was no sidewalk and we lived on a heavily traveled US highway. It was the mid-1960s, and there was a different standard of "watching your child." I freely drank from the garden hose, so walking down the shoulder of a major highway by myself may have been perfectly normal.

My mother says I loved my Sunday school teacher, although my memories are vague. I remember being picked up by an older lady, outside the house we moved to in 1965, in the village of Avoca, several miles from the Wallace church. My first clear memory of the church was when I dutifully picked up my high school graduation bible. I still belonged because my grandparents belonged.

I preached at the Wallace church one Sunday after my ordination as a deacon in The Episcopal Church in 1989. My grandparents were proud but still vocally puzzled about why I would choose a church other than "what I had grown up with," by which they meant Methodism. Of course, I hadn't grown up with it at all. I don't remember my grandparents ever inviting me to church. I have a sense (that no one can corroborate) that there were many years they themselves did not go. Other than that, I chalk it up to a cultural reticence about religion. Our region of upstate New York is called "the burned-over district," due to the late eighteenth- and early nineteenth-century religious fervor in the area, which was responsible for creating the Methodist churches in every little town. The era also produced the Millerites, Mormons, Shakers, and other communal societies.

Yet The Episcopal Church was very foreign to my grandparents. They did not understand it, and they did not seem to want to understand it. At their home later that day, my grandmother handed me a nineteenth-century edition of the Book of Common Prayer, saying, "I think this belongs to your church. I don't know how it got into my attic." (I later learned my grandfather had an uncle who was an Episcopalian.)

I had a glimpse of the past on my preaching visit. I stood by the font to say a little thank-you for my baptism, when the yellow light streaming onto the font from the window shimmered. I felt a strong connection to a memory then, although I could not get to the memory itself. I was overwhelmed by a renewed sense of grace. Something had happened here, something that resonated deep down. Despite the lack of actual memory, I knew what had happened was not primarily something my parents or grandparents did, or the minister, or even me. It was God. It was what we mean by the word "grace." It was a promise made to me and a claim made on me out of the unconditional love of God.

Sometime not long after that incident, I read the novel *Oldest Living Confederate Widow Tells All* by Allan Gurganus. Oddly enough, it was a gift from a friend on the occasion of my ordination as a priest in early January 1990. At the end of a passage in which the old widow is wrestling with the meaning of history, she paraphrases Goethe, comparing history to a prism: "The deeds and sufferings of light make colors. By the time sunlight reaches us, it is beautiful old news. We get tanned, healed, fed by the sun's own long spent ricochet history."[1] I never read that passage without being stunned, taken back to the presence of shimmering light and the memory that stays hidden, of the grace that, like history itself, ricochets between resonance and obscurity, becoming increasingly real over time.

As much as establishing any relationship with God, my baptism rooted me in a place and time, among a particular and peculiar people. I loved my grandparents dearly. They were salt-of-the-earth folks, but more than that. They cared about family, and they cared about community. My Grandfather Hopkins especially taught me to love that place, the Cohocton River valley, and the wide spot in the road called Wallace, and Avoca, the nearby village where generations of my family went to school. They left me the legacy that where I came from and who I came from mattered. More than that, the community and how we lived together was important. Deeply.

The realization of being rooted in a place and time leads me to larger questions about the connection between faith and place. What are the implications of this rootedness and our commitment to the planet and the cosmos? Is there in baptism a fundamental reality that the earth is not something which is simply passing away, a stage on which we live that in the end will have relatively little importance? The clue to answering that question may be in water itself. It is, after all, the most essential element for life. Can it be a coincidence that water is what initiates the Christian life?

We can take another step from these questions and my experience of rootedness. Being bound to a particular place—and through that place to the whole cosmos—is about belonging. I have a place in creation that is at the same time a universal reality and a very particular one. My baptism witnesses that I belong in the cosmos, fashioned out of that cosmos by a hand not my own. My being is intentional. I belong here and now.

So, my baptism was an act of belonging. I can't say that my four-year-old self had a sense of this truth, but it is a value that became important to me later in life. Like many young people from rural areas, I longed to know more of the world. My first taste of this was college. Although I went to one of the many New York State public colleges, I picked one as far away as I could get—an eight-hour drive. Yet I was surprised by the pull my hometown and family continued to have on me. I was genuinely homesick.

In my second semester, in an American history course, the professor assigned a project involving our family of origin and its place in history. A part of the project was to learn as much as we could about our family's past. Despite my strong connections with my family and its place, I knew very little about its past. I set my grandparents to the task of providing me with genealogies and any stories they had about our ancestors. It was the beginning of a lifelong love of genealogy, and it had the effect in that moment of connecting me more deeply with a past I thought I had been trying to escape. I discovered it wasn't an "either-or." I could live somewhere else in an evolving sense of self and still be connected to and nurtured by my roots.

The sense of belonging was vitally important to me as I worked out my sexuality and its relationship to my life in the church. I found belonging in the church quite strongly—here were people who genuinely cared for me and with whom I felt connected. It was, in one sense, a break from my past. Any relationship I had with the church at the time of my baptism had soon dwindled away to nothing. But there were in my roots strong values of faithfulness and duty that translated easily into church membership and faith in God.

When I came out as a gay man in my first year of seminary, my roots already ran deep, and I never struggled with any sense that I somehow didn't belong. In fact, it was that conviction of belonging that carried me through some very difficult days when many around me were questioning it. Because of this experience, I came to understand the gospel—and preach it—as having a great deal to do with belonging. I will come back to this understanding throughout this book. Suffice to say I grew to believe that my baptism, so dim in memory, did not have "little to do" with my relationship with God, as I sometimes wondered in my younger years. It had everything to do with it.

The Book of Common Prayer says that baptism causes an "indissoluble bond" with God and God's Church, a belonging that cannot be broken.[2] I believe the grace of this "indissoluble bond" is equally with God and my neighbor, whoever that neighbor happens to be, and wherever that neighbor happens to be. It is a bond locally, but also a bond globally. It is a bond in the present time, but also in all time. Former Archbishop of Canterbury Rowan Williams has said, "Baptism catches us up in solidarities not of our own choosing."[3] We are united with those who are easy for us to love, and those with whom it is hard to do so. We are united with people who are like us, and with those who are different from us, even those with whom we vehemently disagree. We are all one messy family.

It is because of this gradual epiphany of grace that occurs in the very history of our lives that I know that baptism has both public meaning and public implication. This truth needs unpacking, and I know that some reading this reflection will want to say that I am guilty of a confusion of categories: sacred vs. secular. But there are questions to ask: Does the sacred only reveal itself occasionally in history, or is history itself sacred? If the latter is true, then the sacred, and our participation in it, is messier than we can imagine, certainly more than we would like.

For Christians, I have learned it is not history that is so important as remembering. Remembering is not simply about the past. In remembering we bring three moments together: what is remembered, the present moment, and our anxieties and/or hopes for the future. Remembering shapes present experience, but not in such a way as simply to repeat itself. To truly remember is not to engage in nostalgia, which is a form of idolatry—the holding up of an idealized past by which all presents and futures are to be measured. Nor is it as simple as "learning from the past." It is experiential. It is remembering the past so that the past can participate in making the present. One might say that remembering aids the evolving of the present. This "evolving" is ever moving into a future. It projects, envisions a future.

When I was a boy and into my teenage years, my baptism was something of which I thought little. It was "in the past," over and done. It had no effect on the present that I could see. In the oversimplicity of adolescent thinking, I assumed the past would stay in the past, and I longed for a future that would break from it. I didn't want to be constrained by my family or the little town in which I lived. In the words of one of the greatest of human illusions, I wanted to "make something of myself." It wasn't until much later in life that reality finally came to bear on me; I couldn't make myself alone. People and events in my past were forever part of my journey. Even people and events of which I had no memory were there, ready to help me understand myself and forge a way into a future over which I had less control than I expected.

The Book of Common Prayer's statement about the purpose and effect of baptism echoes my thoughts on these human ties, albeit more succinctly: "Holy Baptism is full initiation by water and the Holy Spirit into Christ's Body the Church. The bond which God establishes in Baptism is indissoluble."[4]

"Full initiation" and "indissoluble bond." More than lovely words, these are asserted as a new dimension of human history. This new dimension plays with time. A future determination impinges upon the present reality. Initiation and bond are not to be earned over a lifetime. They are realized as the fundamental truth about a human being outside of that person's history. At any moment of our history, perhaps especially when we fall short or miss the mark, they remain true. We can utterly fail and they abide. This is the Good News: Our human history does not determine our worth. Our worth is sealed in a new divine dimension.

Time is not only chronological, that is, one minute follows another, one year follows another. Time is also spiritual, that is, living in chronological time we can experience *kairos*, the fullness of time, when the distinctions between past, present, and future blur. The principal reason this is true leaps out of those baptismal superlatives: *full* initiation and *indissoluble* bond. Both proclaim a clear understanding of how the world works, and that is by relationship. Relationship saves us, makes us whole. And this is beyond a necessary relationship with God, or with the Christian Church. Baptism's effect does not stop there. Baptism immerses us in what we might call "deep time," a time in which the past, present, and future are not distinct linear entities, a time in which the divine need not make an appearance on an occasion, but in which the divine simply is. We cannot compartmentalize deep time. We cannot break off pieces of our experience, such as our political activities, and pretend they somehow exist outside of the realm of sacred time.

Some time ago, I attended a town hall meeting for our congressman. He told a joke that I have since then heard politicians and comics tell on other occasions. He said, "You know the definition of politics. It's made up of *poly*, which means 'many,' and *tics*, which are blood-sucking insects." The practice of politics has come to this caricature in our day: politicians attempting to deny that they are politicians. The joke is popular right now because the words "politics" and "politicians" have developed almost completely negative connotations.

What is the responsibility of a Christian in public life? What do words like politics and economics mean for a Christian? What does participation in the public life of the nation, or of the world, have to do with what Bishop Michael Curry, the head of The Episcopal Church, calls, "participating in the Jesus Movement"? He proclaims that to follow Jesus is to follow his way of life, his way of love. This way of talking about the church de-emphasizes the church as institution, establishment, and purveyor of harm, including the harm of white supremacy. "By God's grace," he says, "we are becoming a church that looks and acts like Jesus."[5]

One place to go in search of answers to the questions about Christian responsibility is the Jesus Movement's earliest days, when Christianity was not a culturally acceptable form of religion, but a chosen way of life that could put one in great danger.

CHAPTER 2

The Mystery of
the New People

You should not be greedy nor rapacious nor hypocritical; nor malicious nor proud; and you are not to plan evil against your neighbor.

—*The Didache*, first or second century, CE

Julius and Priscilla sat in the candlelight, waiting for the moment for which they had been preparing for more than two years. They were in the hall of a great house, keeping vigil through the night until the dawn of Easter morning. They were sitting with seven others, listening to the great stories of the scriptures, waiting for baptism. With them were their sponsors who had journeyed with them. Their primary catechist, Quadratus, was among the priests who, with their bishop, were leading the service. Julius and Priscilla shivered in the cold since they were clad in only rough robes that could easily be removed when the time came, for they would enter their new life naked as they had entered their old one.

They were slaves of a Roman official in Nicomedia, the capital of the province of Bithynia in northern Anatolia (Asia Minor). Both had been born into slavery. Fellow slaves from another household convinced them over time to seek incorporation into the local body of Christians.

They had been hesitant. There was danger involved. Off and on local Roman officials—sometimes with direction from Rome and sometimes on their own whim—led persecutions of Christians. Many Bithynian Christians had been put to death when they refused to renounce their faith. The worst of these times had been under Pliny, the Roman governor of Bithynia and Pontus. To the great relief of local Christians, Pliny died in 113 CE, and the persecutions ebbed in the years that followed. Still, the danger remained, and Christians met and worshipped in as much secrecy as possible.

Quadratus and the other catechists had taught them well. For over a year they gathered on Sundays with the rest of the assembly and heard the scriptures proclaimed, after which they, the catechumens (i.e., "the ones being taught"), were dismissed with prayer, and met with the catechists in another room of the house. As Julius and Priscilla understood it, there were three main teachings: that God is One, that Jesus had come as God's child and lived an earthly life, and that following Jesus changed the way they lived in the world. Recently Quadratus had written a letter to a Roman official and shown portions of it to them. He addressed the letter to "Diognetus," a latinized name meaning "born of God." In the opening of the letter, he wrote what he had said to them over and over again: "Clear the thoughts that take up your attention, and pack away all the old ways of looking at things that keep deceiving you. You must become like a new person from the beginning, since you are listening to a really new message."[1]

Quadratus emphasized that as they were learning, they were becoming a new people, a new race.[2] Their baptisms would seal this becoming and they would then be the soul of the world. "What the soul is in the body, that Christians are to the world," was a favorite saying of his.[3] Christians are called to be the world's conscience and, through that conscience, act to build the reign of God on earth as it is in heaven, often in subtle ways, but which, nevertheless, make a difference in personal relationships and, through them, relationships within the whole community.

The One God they were called to worship and serve, the Creator of the universe and the maker of all things, including, as creation's crown, men and women, is kind and good, slow to anger and true. God alone, indeed, is goodness and truth. He has shown us all these things in his child, Jesus. At this point in his lectures (a point he returned to again and again), Quadratus would speak as if he were being directly inspired by the Spirit of God, or so it seemed to them.

O the overflowing kindness and love of God toward humanity! God did not hate us, or drive us away, or bear us ill will. Did he send [Jesus], as a human mind might assume, to rule out of tyranny, fear, and terror? Far from it! He sent him as God; he sent him as a man to humanity. He willed to save us by persuasion, not by compulsion, for compulsion is not God's way of working. He sent him in love, not in judgment. In his mercy he took up the burden of our sins. He himself gave up his own Child as a ransom for us—the holy one for the unjust, the innocent for the guilty, the righteous for the unrighteous. O sweetest exchange! O unfathomable work of God! O blessings beyond expectations! He showed the Savior's power to save even the powerless, with the intention that we should have faith in his goodness and look on him as Nurse, Father, Teacher, Counselor, Healer, Mind, Light, Honor, Glory, Might, Life.[4]

These magnificent words were, for a long time, hard for Julius and Priscilla to hear. Most of their lives they had accepted that the gods were many, capricious, and demanding. At all times they needed to be appeased. It was relatively easy to accept that God was one and not many, but to understand that the one God was creative, merciful, and loving took more time. That God saved not by compulsion but by persuasion was almost incomprehensible.

This good news—as they came to call it—was not only about God. It was also about them—that their status as slaves was meaningless to God. In Jesus, they were taught, they were all brothers and sisters, equal in the sight of God. "We are all one in Christ," Quadratus said, despite the distinctions made between them in the everyday world around them. They learned over time that this reality had far-reaching consequences for how they were to live their lives in the power of God's Spirit.

The teachings of Jesus on this way of living were astounding and clear. Love all, including our enemies, those who curse us, persecute or oppress us. To do this is to be children of God, our loving Father. When struck we are not to strike back; when robbed we are not to sue; when asked to give, to do so gladly, offering more than asked. These are not the ways of the world, where hatred for enemies is given as a most natural thing. If we found ourselves at odds with our neighbor, we seek reconciliation. We love our neighbors as we love ourselves. To do so is to imitate the God they knew in the story of Jesus. Quadratus taught, "Do not be surprised that a man can become an imitator of God. He can, because God wills it."[5]

It would be a lie if they said that they were no longer afraid. Following the way of Jesus could make one conspicuous, as it was such a different way than was followed in the world in which they lived. Luckily their mistress, though not a Christian herself, was sympathetic and protective of her slaves who were. And they had been taught to be good citizens,[6] only abstaining, as much as was possible, from food sacrificed to idols and not participating in the rites of the pagan gods. The former could be difficult, but the latter was relatively easy, as slaves did not often participate in such rites, unless having to accompany their master, which was unusual.

They had not been told about what would happen to them that night, except that it was the entrance into the way of life they sought. Neither did they know what the assembly did after they were dismissed each Sunday. They knew they prayed, and they knew there was some kind of eating, but Quadratus said it was best to experience these things before being taught about them. He did say they would be illuminated, filled with the light and knowledge of the One God and his holy child Jesus. What exactly this meant he would not say, but their friends who had already been baptized described it as having new eyes that saw the world in a new way.

It was time. Priscilla went first because modesty demanded that women and men were baptized separately. Julius would not see her until they both joined the full assembly. She seemed anxious. He smiled and pointed to his eyes. She nodded and was taken away. Several minutes passed before it was his turn. There were four men to be baptized. Upon entering the room, they were stripped of their clothing and oil was poured over their heads. The deacons rubbed the oil into their bodies as the bishop prayed. Julius would remember only snatches of the prayer: "Come power of grace . . . come, perfect mercy . . . revealer of hidden mysteries . . . Spirit of holiness, purify their hearts."[7]

One by one they were turned to the west and asked to renounce Satan and his works. Then they were turned toward the east—the direction from which Christ will come again—and declared him to be their true Lord and Savior. A deacon then took Julius down into a shallow pool of water. The bishop poured water over his head and said he was baptized in the Name of the Father, Son, and Holy Spirit. When he came out of the water the bishop laid hands on him and poured more oil on his head, this oil heavily perfumed, and said, "This is the seal, for you share in the forgiveness of sins. Glory to you, hidden one, who are given in baptism. Glory to you, the unseen power that exists in baptism. Glory to you, renewal, whereby the baptized are renewed and with affection take hold over you."[8]

After this the deacons wiped them down and clothed them with new white robes and they were led back into the main room of the assembly. Priscilla and the other women were there. They were kept separated, but Julius could see all anxiety was gone from her and she looked truly radiant, which was how he himself also felt. The assembly was in prayer, but it ended soon after they arrived and the bishop declared, "Peace be with you. Greet the newly illuminated with the kiss of peace." And one by one, with each of them, that is what they did.

Then bread and wine were brought to the bishop. The deacons spread a linen cloth on a table and the bread and wine were placed on it, and the bishop prayed over these gifts, in words, again, of which Julius only remembered pieces: "Come, perfect love. Come, communion with all humankind. Come, those who share in the mysteries of the Chosen One. Bread of life—those who eat it will remain incorruptible. We drink the Blood that was shed for our salvation. Upon you we invoke the name of your Jesus." When they approached to receive this bread and wine, the bishop said to them "May this Eucharist be unto you for the salvation and joy and health of your souls." They said, "Amen," as they had heard others do. And Priscilla heard the voice of Quadratus, after she had received communion, say, "Amen. Fear not. Just believe."[9]

CHAPTER 3

The Way of Covenant

The God of creation needed to be in relationship . . . The Hebrews dared the paradox of vulnerable perfection, incomplete completeness. God needed God's creation.
—Verna Dozier, *The Dream of God*

By the time Julius and Priscilla were baptized and had participated in their first Eucharist, they would have known that they now belonged to a people—a new people—who practiced a way of life that was the ongoing story of God's relationship with his people. The Christian scriptures had not yet been solidified into an authorized canon; indeed, some of those writings were still in progress. I think they were lucky to have lived in this in-between period. I suspect it was easier to experience themselves as part of an ongoing story. They were, after all, still close in time to Jesus himself, and to the original witnesses to his life. They also lived in a period when the Christian way of life was not a cultural assumption. It was a way that had to be chosen and, once chosen, put one in a decidedly minority and risky position.[1]

It was, of course, inevitable that Christian writings would eventually be assembled into a canon, as had been done to the Hebrew Scriptures before them. It was also inevitable that canon would eventually be closed. For the story to continue there had to be a certain level of agreement on the story's origin. If anything, it is remarkable that there is so much variation in the Gospels in particular. But once this closure happened, "The Scriptures" became an objective thing, something to believe in rather than be lived out.[2] "Does your Church believe in the Bible?" is a question I get asked from time to time. Sometimes when I am feeling bold enough, I say, "No. We believe in God and in the Word of God who is Jesus Christ and in the Holy Spirit who leads us into all truth." That erudition never gets me anywhere, because the follow-up is usually to ask the question again: "But do you believe in the Bible?" Increasingly it seems to me to be wisest to say, "We believe in the Story."

* * *

At the heart of the scriptures is a story, a story of people in the world, in *their* world, in relationship with God and one another. They get it right sometimes; they get it wrong just as often. God loves them; God is angry with them. They are in love with God, but often they wonder if God is on their side or not, and sometimes they themselves are just as angry with God as God is with them. Like any relationship known to humankind, it can be simple and clear one moment and complex and mysterious the next.

This story is at the heart of baptism. Baptism is part of the story. Rather than starting at the beginning of the baptismal rite and traveling in a linear way to its end, I want to start in the middle, because in the middle is where the story comes to the fore.

We thank you, Almighty God, for the gift of water. Over it the Holy Spirit moved at the beginning of creation. Through it you led the children of Israel out of their bondage in Egypt into the land of promise.

These are the opening words of the "Thanksgiving over the Water" (The Book of Common Prayer, p. 306). It references two events from the Old Testament: the creation and the Exodus. It is the Exodus story that is primary here, and if you want further evidence of that primacy note that at the most important time for baptism—the Great Vigil of Easter—of all the Old Testament readings that may be used, only one is required: the Exodus story. The great song near the beginning of the Easter Vigil, known as the Exsultet, also makes reference to this core story (p. 287).

This is the night when you brought our fathers [and mothers], the children of Israel, out of bondage in Egypt, and led them through the Red Sea on dry land.

The Exodus, and the covenant between God and God's people forged in that event and the wilderness journey that followed, is the core story of the Old Testament. Therefore, it is a core story for us, a story of which we are a part: *This is the night.* It is a spiritual story, but also a political story, a story of gaining freedom from oppression and slavery, a story of God acting in history that affects the day-to-day life of people. The story is also an economic one, moving from the economics of scarcity and anxiety under Pharaoh, the endless work of many to the great benefit of the few, to the economics of abundance and the common good.

This whole story is summarized by the word "covenant," a word also used in baptism. The Prayer Book speaks of the Baptismal Covenant, specifically the rehearsal of the Apostles' Creed and the answering of five questions about Christian living. Baptism as a whole, however, *is* a covenant. We need to explore more deeply the meaning of this word "covenant," so to better understand the nature of the promises we made (or that were made for us) in baptism, and which we reaffirm whenever we participate in the baptism of another. What are the responsibilities inherent in our covenant with God?

Covenant as used in the Hebrew Scriptures describes not an agreement or contract, but the promise of fidelity in a relationship. It is not simply a matter of "if you do such-and-such then I will do such-and-such," although there are places the word is used in the scriptures where it sounds like this kind of *quid pro quo* agreement. The primary enactment of covenant is at Mount Sinai with the giving of the Ten Commandments (Exodus 19–24), an event which follows directly upon the Exodus. The whole story of Exodus–Mt. Sinai begins when God hears the cry of the Israelites living in bondage:

The Israelites groaned under their slavery, and cried out. Out of the slavery their cry for help rose up to God. God heard their groaning, and God remembered his covenant with Abraham, Isaac, and Jacob. God looked upon the Israelites, and God took notice of them. (Exodus 2:23–25)

The Exodus–Mt. Sinai covenant has its roots in previous covenants God made with individuals, with Noah "and all flesh"

(Genesis 9) and with Abraham and his offspring (Genesis 15 and 17). These covenants, however, are but the background of the new thing God is doing with Israel. The Exodus–Mt. Sinai covenant is a promise of fidelity and of steadfast love between God and his chosen people. This covenant is not *quid pro quo*, although it does come with absolute commands, which we know as the Ten Commandments. These are more than "commands" as we tend to use the word, however. They are more than rules to be followed. They are a description of how the relationship between God and God's people will work, and, in turn, how relationships will work within the covenant community. One can see this in the term that is used for the Ten Commandments in the Hebrew Scriptures: They are the Ten Words, "word" being a term denoting creativity. One can also see it in the Hebrew term for the ongoing interpretation of these "Ten Words" (and the 613 other commandments that Jews find in the Torah)—*halakah*, "the path one walks," or "the way." Just the notion that there needs to be ongoing interpretation is instructive. Overall, because this covenant is about relationship, there will be some messiness, often requiring renewed understanding.

The scriptures speak first of God's everlasting covenant that cannot be changed, despite Israel's disobedience and God's righteous anger. This promise of fidelity was an aspect of both Genesis covenants. God says to Noah, "When the bow is in the clouds, I will see it and remember the everlasting covenant between God and every living creature of all flesh that is on the earth" (Genesis 9:16). And to Abraham, God says, "I will establish my covenant between me and you and your offspring after you throughout their generations, for an everlasting covenant, to be God to you, and to your offspring" (Genesis 17:8).

Yet the Exodus–Mt. Sinai covenant comes with conditions. If the commands are violated *as a nation,* life will become unbearable for Israel. They will live under curse rather than blessing. Perhaps the clearest expression of this reality is in Deuteronomy 30: "If you obey the commandments of the Lord your God that I am commanding you today, by loving the Lord your God, walking in his ways, and observing his commandments, decrees, and ordinances, then you shall live and become numerous, and the Lord your God will bless you in the land." The address is not to individuals but to the nation.

If at this point it sounds like the covenant has become *quid pro quo,* there is a sense in which it has. But as the story unfolds, it is not so simple for God, whose rejection of the people for their disobedience is never complete. God's steadfast love for the people remains as the most important promise, a promise that ultimately triumphs over any judgment. God has created a people who infuriate him frequently, but of whom he cannot let go, cannot abandon. This is true even for that part of the story that is all about abandonment—the Exile.

* * *

If Exodus–Mt. Sinai is a central event for the Hebrew Scriptures, it is actually one of two poles, the other being the Exile, the most profound experience of abandonment, of God's turning away from Israel.

Yet even this abandonment, as real an experience of God's judgment as Israel knew, is temporary in Israel's memory. The prophet Isaiah, near the end of the exile, speaks of "a brief moment" of abandonment which will be overcome by God's "great compassion," and the return to relationship that will bring about renewed promises of an "everlasting covenant" (Isaiah 55:3; 61:8). Indeed, the prophet Jeremiah had predicted this while the destruction of Jerusalem was taking place, and, even amidst the harsh blame he placed on his exiled people, he prophesied of a coming newness:

> The days are surely coming, says the LORD, when I will make a new covenant with the house of Judah. It will not be like the covenant that I made with their ancestors when I took them by the hand to bring them out of the land of Egypt—a covenant that they broke, though I was their husband, says the LORD. But this is the covenant that I will make with the house of Israel after those days, says the LORD: I will put my law within them, and I will write it on their hearts; and I will be their God and they will be my people (Jer. 31:31–33).

This odd juxtaposition of promise and abandonment speaks to a larger reality that is easy to forget as one reads these scriptures. Most scholars believe that a large portion of the Hebrew Scriptures found their definitive form *during exile*. Israel understood, says Old Testament scholar Walter Brueggemann, that the broken covenant was "not termination but eclipse."[3]

The nature of covenant is twofold: Not two opposites, but two complements. The acceptance by God is absolute, but so is

God's insistence on a way of life (*halakah*). The insistence of God is non-negotiable for Israel, but so is the deep knowledge of God's acceptance, God's steadfast love. Again, this is not a contract that is either/or. This is a covenant which is both/and. It was not easy for Israel to understand it or to live it out. It is still not easy for the people of God to do so. Perhaps what Jeremiah meant by God's desire to write the law on the hearts of the people was just this: For Israel to know both the absolute insistence and the deep acceptance. Knowing both is the only way for God and God's people truly to love and trust each other.

The covenant is also both political and pragmatic, affectional and passionate. Brueggemann writes of this reality: There is, he says, both a political/economic and an affective dimension to covenant living, with love being what keeps the tension alive.

> The obligation of Israel to Yahweh is to love Yahweh. . . . Love is a dense term. Clearly it is a covenant word that means to acknowledge sovereignty and to keep one's loyalty, on which the covenant is based. But such a political dimension of the term does not rule out an affective dimension, in light of the term set one's heart (hsq) . . . Thus at the core of Israel's obligation to Yahweh is the desire to please Yahweh and to be with Yahweh (Psalms. 27:4, 73:25). This dimension of desire and joy is what, in the best construal, keeps Israel's obligation to Yahweh from being a burden.[4]

Despite the crucial elements of love and desire, though, the covenant at the heart of Israel's life was not solely spiritual in nature. It governed all of Israel's life. It was, in fact, far more public than private. Of course, it did impinge on the lives of individuals, but it was first and foremost a covenant with the nation, defining its public, political, and economic life. What were Israel's obligations under this covenant, and what does that tell us about the meaning of such terms as "politics?" Again, Brueggemann writes:

> Israel's obligation is to do justice. Israel is a community put into the world . . . for the sake of justice. The justice commanded by Yahweh, moreover, is not the retributive justice of "deeds—consequences" wherein rewards and punishments are meted out to persons and the community according to conduct. Rather, Israel understands itself . . . as a community of persons bound in membership to each other, so that each person as member is to be treated well enough to be sustained as a full member of the community. . . . the wealth and social resources of Israel are understood not in a privatistic or acquisitive way, but as common resources that are to be managed and deployed for the advancement of the community by the enhancement of its weakest members.[5]

The bond of community is as strong as the bond with God. This will eventually be expressed as the twin "summary" commandments to love God and to love neighbor, commands present in the story itself (Deut. 6:5; Lev. 19:18), and later proclaimed by Jesus (Matt. 22:35–40; Mark 12:28–31; Luke 10:25–28).

The communal and public nature of covenant can be examined more closely by looking at the fourth commandment, the keeping of Sabbath. Sabbath-keeping has devolved for most Christians into an impractical expression of piety. In truth, for most of us, Sabbath (whether you think of it as Saturday or Sunday) is a day to "get things done." Taking the time to worship on Sunday is the only bow to Sabbath that most of us make. Yet this is not the biblical vision of Sabbath.

Coming after the Exodus experience of slavery under the government of Pharaoh, Sabbath enacted the communal resistance to the values of that government. Pharaoh's claim to absolute authority was built on the practice of endless anxiety, chiefly the anxiety of scarcity. In a land dominated by Pharaoh's bottomless need for self-aggrandizement and increasingly scarce labor to feed it, slavery became the option for the making of bricks to fuel Pharaoh's building projects.

Into the total dominance of Pharaoh, an alternative word was spoken, a word brought to life by the groaning of the people. God says, "I hear your cry and come to rescue you. I who formed you as my people Israel declare my sovereignty over you. I reject the sovereignty of Pharaoh."

In the Ten Commandments, God reasserts priority over Pharaoh and Pharaoh's values. In the first three commandments, establishing the sole reign of God, one might hear an echo of Pharaoh's exclusivist claims. But God goes beyond Pharaoh by establishing the practice of neighborliness in commandments five through ten. Right relationship with God—unlike right relationship with Pharaoh—requires right relationship with neighbor. Relationship with Pharaoh was always vertical; relationship with God is both vertical and horizontal.

The Sabbath commandment is the hinge between these two poles of God and neighbor. Its critical importance is displayed by its inordinate length. It is the longest of the ten and the one that directly references both the people's creation and their experience of slavery. It provides something Pharaoh never provided—rest. The rest serves to turn the anxiety that undergirded Pharaoh's rule into the simple enjoyment of God and creation to nourish well-being.

Brueggemann summarizes the Sabbath commandment in this way:

> Rest as did your creator God! And while you rest be sure that your neighbors rest alongside you. Indeed, sponsor a *system of rest* that contradicts the *system of anxiety* of Pharaoh, because you are no longer subject to Pharaoh's anxiety system.[6]

Imagine a "system of rest!"

Some will remember days when the Sabbath commandment (in particular) was supported by law in the United States, although it was the so-called Christian Sabbath (i.e., Sunday) when shops were closed and activities other than church service highly discouraged. Nostalgia for these days is understandable, especially as employment, shopping, and athletic or other social events impinge upon church attendance. Yet in some ways those laws did the notion of Sabbath more harm than good. It made Sabbath into a law and social convention that had to be followed, rather than a key part of a way of life that must be chosen.

God's covenant with Israel was an intentional commitment to an exclusive relationship with God, lived out in God's steadfast promise of faithfulness and the practice of neighborliness, a practice based not on anxiety but on the desire for *shalom*, well-being for all. One can hear this dynamic in the description of the covenant of baptism from the Book of Common Prayer: "Holy Baptism is full initiation by water and the Holy Spirit into Christ's Body the Church. The bond which God establishes in Baptism is indissoluble" (p. 298). If nothing else, this is a description of life lived with God which is not driven by anxiety about the stability of one's relationship with God or with neighbor in the Body of Christ. Among the questions with which we will wrestle through the rest of this book is what other than anxiety drives our relationship with God and one another.

* * *

It is important to ask at this point, "What about the New Covenant?" Does Israel's covenant with God still apply? Did not Jesus replace it? Aren't the Old and New Covenants based on entirely different principles, that is law and grace?

That Jesus replaced the Old Covenant based on law with the New Covenant based on grace has been a kind of Christian shorthand for how Jesus and the Christians who follow him relate to God differently than their Jewish ancestors (or contemporaries). Unfortunately, this shorthand has caused much misunderstanding of the relationship between Jews and Christians (at best) and anti-Semitic evil (at worst).

There is a shorthand answer to this problem: Grace is not absent from the covenant with our Jewish ancestors, and law/obedience is not absent from the covenant Jesus says he is making "with his blood." In fact, in both Matthew and Mark, Jesus says at the Last Supper, "This is my blood of the covenant, which is poured out for many" (Matt. 26:28; Mark 14:24). It is Luke who adds the word "new" to Jesus's words, as does Paul in his remembrance of the words (1 Cor. 11:25). They were, perhaps, deliberately tying Jesus's words to those of Jeremiah. Most Christians are surprised to hear this since the words, "This is my blood of the *new* covenant (or testament)" has for centuries been the norm for the Words of Institution recited as part of the Eucharist.

This "old vs. new" dynamic is reinforced by some New Testament texts. The prologue to John's Gospel says, "The law indeed was given through Moses; grace and truth came through Jesus Christ" (John 1:17). Paul's dichotomy between faith and works, that it is faith that saves us rather than works of following the law, provides even more fodder. This is not the place for a long excursus on this debate, however, so I'll say three things that will hopefully move us forward:

1. Jesus never repudiates the Exodus–Mt. Sinai covenant. He is critical of certain aspects of the law, but also says he has not come "to abolish the law or the prophets; I have come not to abolish but to fulfill" (Matt. 5:17). His critique of the law might be summarized in his comments about Sabbath observance: "The sabbath was made for humankind, and not humankind for the sabbath" (Mark 2:27). The law was not made simply for

obedience to God. It was made for the well-being of women and men in neighborly common good.

2. It is impossible (and a worthless exercise) to parse the difference between the concept of *ḥesed* (steadfast love) in the Old Testament and *charis* (grace) in the New Testament. A core Christian principle is that God loves us first (1 John 4:19; John 15:16). That God chose Israel before Israel chose God (and repeatedly so) is just as fundamental to the Old Testament. If there is anything "new" about the New Covenant, it is the expansion of the chosen people to include all people, Jews and Gentiles. And yet even this expansion was encouraged in the Old Testament. Israel was to be a light to the nations, and the nations, it was predicted, would stream to the God of Israel.

3. Jesus's living out the covenant and leaving commands for his disciples is not a solely spiritual enterprise, or, perhaps, it is better put that Jesus's life and the way of life he offers his followers does not limit the spiritual to the private and personal relationship with God and the believer whose goal is an other-worldly heaven. No, Jesus commands that we love one another now and he teaches us to pray for God's kingdom to come "on earth as it is in heaven."

As we proceed, we will look for ways that the Baptismal Covenant is an expression of God's continuing call for God's people to live in covenant relationship with God and with neighbor. As we continue to tell the story and live it in our daily lives, it remains both private and public, affective and political/economic.

CHAPTER 4

The Way of Turning

When true simplicity is gained to bow and to bend we shan't be ashamed, to turn, turn, will be our delight till by turning, turning, we come round right.

—Eighteenth century Shaker Song
(attr. to Joseph Bracket)

The Shakers' origin was in late eighteenth century England, but they quickly spread to the newly independent United States, first in upstate New York. They then spread westward to Ohio and Kentucky and eastward to New England. At their most numerous there were some 4,000 of them living in eighteen major communities. Today, only one small community remains in Maine. At first glance, they may not be the best example to use about the public implications of baptism, as they were a people who led a communal life apart from the world as much as possible, and they denounced much of the normative way of living around them, including being married and raising children.[1] The Shakers, however, were convinced that the gospel called them to a particular lifestyle, a particular way of living in society, a way of being in the world. Brother Arnold Hadd, one of the last two Shakers alive, puts it this way, "We are to make life as little hellish for each other as possible."[2] For the Shakers, the way of Jesus was always a way of relationship, of being a society (their official name is "The United Society of Believer's in Christ's Second Appearing"). This way of life in relationship must be deliberately chosen, and living in it meant a constant turning.

The Christian life is about turning, not as a singular event, but as a way of life. The religious word for it is "conversion," but the Latin word behind the English word "conversion" means "turning" or "change." So does the Greek word, although it is usually translated "repent." Yet *metanoia* actually means "to turn around" or "to go in a different direction." So, what does it mean to lead a life of "turning?"

To begin with, one always turns from one thing to another. The baptismal rite, from ancient times, has begun with a turning. The person to be baptized (or their parents and godparents) renounces all evil and turns to Jesus. The current Book of Common Prayer makes a threefold "turning from" matched by a threefold "turning toward."

Question: Do you renounce Satan and all the spiritual forces of wickedness that rebel against God?

Answer: I renounce them.

Question: Do you renounce the evil powers of this world which corrupt and destroy the creatures of God?

Answer: I renounce them.

Question: Do you renounce all sinful desires that draw you from the love of God?

Answer: I renounce them.

Question: Do you turn to Jesus Christ and accept him as your Savior?

Answer: I do.

Question:	Do you put your whole trust in his grace and love?
Answer:	I do.
Question:	Do you promise to follow and obey him as your Lord?

In some places in the early church, this turning was enacted within the rite itself. To renounce evil, those to be baptized faced the west, and some rites called for them to spit in the direction of evil. To turn to faith in Jesus they faced the east, symbolically facing Jerusalem and the direction from which it was believed Jesus would return. Altars were (and still are) normally in the east end of a church building. One should take care to note that the renunciation, although it faces "the world," is not a rejection of the world itself, but of the evil often encountered in the world.

Folks who come to prepare for baptism are often brought up short by the word "Satan" in the renunciations. "Do we really believe in Satan?" I have been asked on many occasions. "Believe in?" I like to reply "No, we save belief for God." Yet Satan is a powerful figure in Christian imagination. The word "sâtân" is Hebrew and means an opponent, accuser, or adversary. It is frequently used in the Hebrew Scriptures to mean just that—an adversary.[3] As Judaism developed, the figure of Satan developed also, eventually becoming a full-blown personality opposed to God and to humanity, but never on a par with God.

As a name, Satan only appears in the Hebrew Scriptures in three places: Job 2, Zechariah 3:1–2, and 1 Chronicles 21:1. The latter is a good example of how the figure developed. Chronicles retells a story about David found in 2 Samuel 24:1. In the first telling of the story, God is angry with Israel and incites David to count the people. In Chronicles, it is Satan who incites David. The earlier version assumes a God who can do both good and evil. By the time the Chronicles were put together, the writers were hesitant to put the incitement of evil in God's hands. Satan became a way to personify evil.

In the New Testament, Satan appears more frequently (sometimes as "the devil," which is not a Hebrew concept), beginning with Jesus's temptation in the wilderness in the Gospels of Matthew, Mark, and Luke.[4] Overall, the most important thing to know about Satan in the New Testament is that he is not victorious in the end and, as in the Hebrew Scriptures, is never put on par with God. Christianity does not divide the world into equal forces of evil and good, who are fighting a cosmic battle. What battle there is, the New Testament proclaims, God has already won.

The fight between good and evil and the "relationship" between God and Satan were issues with which the early church struggled. Many popular religious expressions of the time taught the creation itself was evil, and that the believer's job was to escape from it, usually by being initiated into a secret way of understanding. These sects became known by the Greek word for "knowledge:" *gnosis.* Various Gnostic sects attracted some early Christians because, on their face, they seemed to describe what was obvious, that is, the battle between good and evil. There arose from these sects ways of understanding God's purposes in the world, and the role of Jesus in those purposes, that were eventually identified as heresies. One example was "Docetism," which held that Jesus did not actually become human. He could not do so, in their view, because the flesh was fundamentally evil. He only *appeared* to be human, and it was that appearance that was crucified, not the real Son of God.

It's easy to get hung up on Satan, but, fascinating as he might be, the point of the three renunciations is that evil is a real choice, in the cosmos, in the world, and in one's personal life. In the life of faith, "spiritual forces of wickedness," "the evil powers of this world," and "sinful desires" are very real. They can be chosen, and they can be participated in, either knowingly or unknowingly.

The Confession of Sin in the book of alternative texts for worship in The Episcopal Church (*Enriching Our Worship I*) makes this knowing or unknowing very clear. It includes the statement, "We repent of the evil that enslaves us, the evil we have done, and the evil done on our behalf."[5] My experience when my first parish began using this prayer, was that a number of people balked at this sentence. They did not know what "the evil done on our behalf" meant, and even if they had an inkling what it was, they didn't think they should feel any guilt about it. They said, "It's out of our control. It's not our fault." There was also a general exception to the use of the word "evil," which they assumed was reserved for the truly bad persons who had done especially horrid things, such as murder or the serial physical abuse of others.

But if the Bible knows anything about evil it is its banality, its ordinariness. The things that corrupt and destroy, that draw us from the love of God, are the stuff of ordinary life. They are so much so that we often have trouble recognizing them. That's why a turning is required, a turning that over time sharpens our awareness and our capacity to discern what is good and what is evil, by using the sight that Jesus gives us. This turning is away from separation from God and harm of one another (whether by intention or due to apathy), in order to turn toward what gives life, in faith, hope, and love.

The evil powers of this world which corrupt and destroy the creatures of God are not always obvious. Yet they are endemic to every human system or institution. New Testament scholar Walter Wink says, "The gospel is . . . permanently critical of every political program, reform, or revolution."[6] He goes on to say that because we live in the time when the cycle of creation, fall, and redemption is an ongoing drama, political systems are necessary, even upheld by God, "since some such system is required to support human life." Yet such systems are also under God's judgment, "insofar as [they are] destructive of full human actualization." They are also under God's insistence that they transform "into a more human order."[7]

Neither I nor anyone else has to convince most people that there is evil in our political systems. It is wrong, however, to believe that it is innately so. If it was, humanity would probably have ended itself and creation long ago. The task of people of faith is to learn to see what it is in our political system, or any institution (including the church) that tends toward evil. To do this we need to learn to see not with our own ideological eyes or the eyes of some system of rigid morality (both of which are as subject to evil influence as any other system). We need to do it in the spirit of "turning."

The turnings to Jesus are the essential aspect of this part of the baptismal liturgy. In baptism we are called to turn to Jesus, specifically to him as "Lord" and "Savior," which means first and foremost, as the rite says, placing our trust in his grace and love. There's much spiritual vocabulary in that sentence that needs unpacking!

First, we need to consider the many titles given to Jesus both in the New Testament and over time. They are human titles that come out of historical and cultural contexts. To attribute them to the divine is to use them as metaphors—descriptions that help us understand their object, but never perfectly. They give us insight into God, but God also breaks them, and it is in the breaking that meaning is found. Take for instance, the word "Almighty" used as a title for or attribute of God. In our liturgical prayer, it may be the most common attribute/title given to the divine.[8] St. Paul knows this attribute is broken by God. In 1 Corinthians, near the beginning of the letter, Paul speaks about the cross as "foolishness" and "a stumbling block," and goes on to say, "God's foolishness is wiser than human wisdom, and God's weakness is stronger than human strength" (1 Cor. 1:25). Indeed, a prayer from the Book of Common Prayer picks up on this very brokenness: "O God, you declare your almighty power chiefly in showing mercy and pity . . ."[9]

The same brokenness can be applied to the use of "Lord," "Savior," and "Christ" (as well as the Hebrew "Messiah") as titles for Jesus. Jesus himself uses these terms sparingly. He refers to himself as "Lord" only obliquely, except for one occasion in John's Gospel, in his teaching after he washes the disciples' feet. "You call me Teacher [Rabbi] and Lord—and you are right, for that is what I am." But then he immediately breaks these titles open: "So if I, your Lord and Teacher, have washed your feet, you also ought to wash one another's feet" (John 13:13–14). He has just taken the role of a servant in washing the disciples. Peter recoils from this precisely because what Jesus is doing does not fit his human understanding of "Lord."

Nevertheless, "Lord" was probably the title most-used by others for Jesus in the New Testament and in the early church. It was clearly preferred over "Savior," a title Jesus never uses himself and which can only be found once in the Gospels in reference to him, out of the mouth of those to whom the Samaritan woman bears witness after her encounter with Jesus (John 4:42). He is called savior twice in the Acts of the Apostles: once by Peter (Acts 5:31) and once by Paul (Acts 13:23). It is elsewhere used very sparingly, except in three New Testament writings: the Letters of Titus and Jude and the Second Letter of Peter. These three letters are thought by scholars to be among the last written among the accepted New Testament canon.

The difference in the use of "Lord" versus "Savior" can be understood from historical context. The early Christians used "Lord" more often because its common usage was widespread, including in the Hebrew Scriptures available to them, the Greek Septuagint. In the Septuagint, the Greek *kyrios* ("Lord") was used to translate the Hebrew *'adonai* and also used in place of the divine name YHWH. "Savior" was also used with some frequency, especially in the later Hebrew Scriptures in the context of the hoped-for liberator/messiah.[10] "Savior" (Greek, *soteros*), however, was a term attributed to Roman emperors as a title. It was an essential aspect of the so-called *Pax Romana*, the peaceful era of Roman domination of the various peoples under its rule. Only the empire—and, therefore, the emperor—could save the world from endless conflict. Hence its usage for Jesus developed only over time as Christians grew in number and daring.

All three titles used in the "turning to" questions of the beginning of the baptismal rite—Lord, Savior, and Christ—were expressions of believers' experience of Jesus, although they were, as I have argued above, always broken open for their meaning. They were each of them subversive, in that they were attached to a singular experience of Jesus. Jesus was *the* Lord, *the* Savior, *the* Christ (the latter so much so that from the earliest days it became a part of Jesus's name). Jesus was the one owed singular allegiance and obedience as Lord, the Lord of what Jesus called "the kingdom of God" or the "kingdom of heaven." Human liberation and salvation were only found in relationship to him, and he was the long-awaited Messiah of Jewish hope.

The subversion was not simply to use what were essentially political titles as referencing a spiritual experience. It was also a subversion in the political realm. If Jesus was the Lord, the emperor, or any of his governors and administrators were not. Hundreds of early Christians lost their lives because they refused to call the emperor "Lord," or worship him in some way. And the Christian experience of salvation from the very beginning had both spiritual and political aspects. It was as simple as the twofold commandment to love God and to love one's neighbor. Roman Catholic theologian Edward Schillebeeckx puts the early Christian experience in these terms:

> Some people . . . came into contact with Jesus of Nazareth and stayed with him. This encounter, and what took place in the life of Jesus and in connection with his death, gave their personal lives new meaning and new significance. They felt they had been born again, that they had been understood, and this new identity found expression in a similar solidarity towards others . . . This change in the course of their lives was the result of their encounter with Jesus, for without him they would have remained what they had been. It had not come through any initiative of their own; it had simply happened to them. This astonishing and overwhelming encounter with the man Jesus became the starting-point for the New Testament view of

salvation. To put it plainly "grace" has to be expressed in terms of encounter and experience; it can never be isolated from the specific encounter which brought liberation.[11]

What does it mean to accept salvation from Jesus? To call Jesus, "Savior?" Schillebeeckx's use of the term "liberation" is important in considering an answer to these questions. More conservative-minded folk may be nervous at this use. Aside from the shared linguistic roots of the words "liberation" and "liberal," there is the trend of "liberation theology" over the past forty years, some of which has expressed Marxist theory. But the use of the word "liberation" to express the human experience of salvation, the fruit of a lifelong encounter with the living Christ, is thoroughly biblical and theologically orthodox. When women and men experience Jesus in their lives, they experience freedom. To accept Jesus as Savior, is to accept the freedom that he offers.

What is this experience of freedom? It is broad enough to be manifest uniquely in each and every person, because it is the freedom of human personality. Salvation *is* a personal experience, but it is also a communal one, in that the personal experience is both unique and shared. Christians are never Christians alone. Christian community is the context for the experience of salvation. I am saved uniquely *and* I am saved communally. In addition, salvation is never the end point of experience. It is much better understood as the beginning of a lifetime of encounter with Jesus, a lifetime in which salvation and liberation are experienced again and again, in a way that moves us closer and closer to true freedom in relationship with God. As the Shakers sing, "to turn, turn will be our delight, 'til by turning, turning, we come round right."

This is why Paul can say two seemingly opposite things: "Now is the day of salvation!" he proclaims in 2 Corinthians (6:2), but to the Philippians he says, "Work out your own salvation with fear and trembling" (Phil. 2:12). Salvation is the result of a singular encounter with Christ, and it is also an ongoing experience that requires our attention and intention in daily life.

So, what is the experience of salvation, of liberation, of freedom in Christ? It is at least the overcoming of fear and anxiety. The command not to be afraid, or not to be anxious or worried, is a frequent one throughout the Bible. It occurs at least 108 times in the Old Testament and 57 in the New Testament. Of course, life without fear or anxiety is humanly impossible. Yet freedom from fear and anxiety does not mean they never occur, only that they need not take control. That they do sometimes take control of our lives is simply another reason Paul says we must work out our salvation.

We must take a brief aside to be clear about the other biblical use of the word "fear," and this is in relationship with God. This is the fear Paul means when he says to work out your salvation "in fear and trembling." Proper fear of God is of great biblical importance, mostly in the Old Testament, but also in Paul's writings (though hardly at all in the Gospels). Presbyterian Pastor and theologian Eugene Peterson helps us understand the meaning and importance of this biblical phrase. Its meaning is not simply the definition of "fear" plus the definition of "Lord." Linguistically, he points out, both in Hebrew and in English, it is a "syntagm," that is, words put together that take on a meaning of their own, sometimes referred to as "a bound phrase." "Fear-of-the-Lord," as he puts it, "means something more like a way of life in which human feelings and behavior are fused with God's being and revelation."[12] The human desire for God, God's steadfast love for humankind, the mystery of God's presence, human awe, wonder, and humility, are all part of this biblical paradigm. Understood and experienced in this way, fear-of-the-Lord and the first letter of John's admonition, "There is no fear in love, but perfect love casts out fear" (1 John 4:18), are not opposites, but complementary realities.

To follow Jesus as Lord is to follow in the love that casts out fear, the love whose embrace is of the life of all God has created. Franciscan Richard Rohr writes, "The following of Jesus is not a 'salvation scheme' or a means of creating social order . . . as much as it is *a vocation to share in the fate of God for the life of the world.*"[13] Rohr's use of the word "fate" is important. By the "fate of God" Rohr means God's ultimate will for the creation. To share in that fate, that will, requires courage, fueled not by our own strength or merit, but by the grace of God. I use the word "courage" here not in the sense of heroism or bravado, but in the capacity to step outside oneself, to set aside one's preconceived notions and examine one's life. Courage is the openness to a new way of being.

This new way of being is the way of the cross, the upside-down way where we lose life in order to gain it and embrace death in order to gain victory over it. This is the way of turning, a way in which we are always ready to be surprised, to change our minds so that we might participate in that for which we pray—for the kingdom of God to come on earth as it is in heaven. It is the way of conversion, which is not an event, but a way of living.

All of this could—and does—describe the inner, spiritual work of all people. Yet it also describes the outer, spiritual work required of all of us. To follow Jesus is to follow him into the depths of one's own being *and* into the world. Sin and fear and death must be confronted in both realms. Wink says, "Those who enter the new reality of God receive, not just a new heart and a new spirit, but a transformed relationship to the world, to time, and even to their bodies. That is the pledge of the One who says, 'I am making all things new' (Rev. 21:5)."[14]

The newness that is being made, and which we must constantly turn toward, is the life of love, the life lived when we experience the perfect love that casts out fear. It is expressed in many ways, but chief among them is freedom, liberation, salvation. We must not understand the divine gift of freedom in an individualistic sense. The freedom which God is making among us is the freedom born of equality, the erasure of the many boundaries we put up between people, and the prejudices which our petty judgments allow to live and grow in our own hearts. William Stringfellow, an Episcopal theologian and activist in the 1960s and 1970s, says of baptism:

> "[it] is the sacrament of the extraordinary unity among men *[sic]* wrought by God in overcoming the power and reign of death, in overcoming, that is, all that alienates, segregates, divides, and destroys men in their relations to each other, indeed also within their own person, and in their relationship with the rest of creation."[15]

Roman Catholic pastoral theologian Henri Nouwen describes the turning from sin to the following of Jesus in much the same way: "Living the spiritual life means living life as one unified reality. The forces of darkness are the forces that split, divide, and set in opposition. The forces of light unite. The demon divides; the Spirit unites."[16]

The task of unity as a spiritual and communal mandate from the one we call Lord and Savior shapes the public life of the Christian. It turns away from a commitment to ideology over people, expediency over love. It does not demand particular policies in organizing our common life. Unity is not equal to uniformity. However, the search for unity upholds a purpose which those policies must help to shape: the unity-without-fear which is God's dream for the world. So much of contemporary politics is fear-based and anxiety-driven, and therefore about a particular ideology grasping for or maintaining power over others. The only way forward in the politics of fear is the way of violence, about which we will have much more to say in the next chapter.

Sin is real, but it also can be turned from and left behind. The powers of this world often participate in sin by encouraging an individualistic ethic of "me first," causing us to live in a world driven by judgment that produces the division—often violent—of individuals and groups against other individuals and groups in a phony game of survival of the fittest. In this game those in power are tempted to speak for God rather than to listen for what God is saying. The opposite way is what Jesus called the kingdom of God. This way requires conversion, which means that our public life is always contingent, always seeking more common good and less self-seeking. If Jesus is Savior and Lord for Christians, they must be ready, as Wink says, "to be permanently critical of every political program." This does not mean we stand in the way of progress, but that we maintain a clear vision of what progress must include: the love of neighbor and the dedication to peace and justice to which the Baptismal Covenant commits us. To this covenant we now turn.

CHAPTER 5

The Way That Turns the World Upside Down

Jesus wept when he saw how Jerusalem has been consumed by a culture of death. It is the powers of death that stand in stark opposition to what Jesus cares about and represents, that is, life itself.

—Kelly Brown Douglas, *Stand Your Ground*

W hat is dignity?" the Rev. Thomas Lee Hayes asked as he was preparing me for confirmation. "Think about that and we'll talk about it next time." I well remember the question, although unfortunately I do not remember the ensuing conversation. I was a twenty-year-old college student, and my sessions with Father Hayes were one-on-one, since all the other confirmands were much younger than me.

I did not know at the time that I was being mentored by a giant in the peace and justice movement in The Episcopal Church. Father Hayes was the new rector, and I didn't know much about him except for that he possessed a good humor, a singing voice that could shake the rafters of St. Thomas's Church, and that he wore an odd cross, a cross atop a circle with a peace symbol. Later I learned it was the cross worn by members of the Episcopal Peace

Fellowship. Learning this information helped make sense of the other snippet of wisdom I remember from our sessions together: "Every Christian's life is a fifth gospel. Your life is a witness to the good news." Let's examine the ways in which this can be true, and the sacrifices that often come with those ways.

* * *

Although the notion of the sacrament of baptism as a covenant is ancient, what Episcopalians know as "The Baptismal Covenant" (The Book of Common Prayer, p. 304–305) is new to the current version of the prayer book. Until 1976, the word "covenant," had not been used in relation to baptism in the prayer book tradition since the first book in 1549. By the 1928 Book of Common Prayer, the parallel to the current covenant was three questions:

Dost thou believe in all the Articles of the Christian Faith, as contained in the Apostles' Creed?

Wilt thou be baptized in this Faith?

Wilt thou then obediently keep God's holy will and commandments, and walk in the same all the days of thy life?[1]

The current prayer book replaced these questions with the recital of the entire Apostles' Creed, and added five new questions which add detail to what it means to "obediently keep" and "walk in the same." We will explore the creedal portion of the covenant in this chapter. The word "dignity" does not appear in the Creed, yet it is important to know from the beginning that is where we are headed.

The history of this creed is shrouded in mystery. Attributed to the apostles themselves, it appears to have grown out of the early Church's baptismal practice, which usually featured three questions affirming faith in the members of the Trinity. The title "Apostles' Creed" first shows up in a letter of St. Ambrose dated around 390 CE. The text in its present form isn't found until the early eighth century. Around this same time in the Western church, it found its way into the daily offices. It remains the creed used at Morning and Evening Prayer in the prayer book. There was an intermediate step, often referred to as "The Old Roman Creed." It is more concise and first appears in the *Apostolic Tradition* of the mid-third century.[2]

It might seem that there is no sign of public life in the Apostles' Creed. Yet even in that older version there is the mention of a political figure, Pontius Pilate. His mention serves as an historical marker, signifying that Jesus was crucified *at the time* of Pontius Pilate, an historical figure, prefect (governor) of Roman Judea from 26 to 36 CE. The historian Josephus (*c.* 37-*c.* 100 CE) and philosopher Philo (*c.* 20 BCE-*c.* 50 CE) witness this fact.

Yet the presence of Pilate is more than a simple marker. It says that Jesus's death was tied up in the politics of his day. "Under Pontius Pilate" in the creed certainly means more than "at the time of." Pilate's hands were all over the crucifixion. It was carried out under his imperial authority, with the collaboration of the Jewish high priestly family, who came to see Jesus as a threat to the nation and a blasphemer. Jesus died at the hands of the state, however, as did hundreds of thousands like him. Crucifixion itself was the Roman

Empire's ultimate death penalty for slaves and insurrectionists. Pilate's role in the passion and death of Jesus forever calls attention to and condemns the use of violence to silence men, women, and movements that threaten the authority of both the state and religious institutions.

We have no evidence that Jesus sought to overthrow the state or religious authorities. Yet he was highly critical of them, in particular calling out their hypocrisy. He associated with those labeled "sinners," ate with the disreputable such as tax collectors, touched the sick and allowed the sick to touch him, and healed on the Sabbath. He called King Herod Antipas "that fox" (Luke 13:32) and told Pilate that he had no authority over him that had not been granted from above (John 19:11).

If Jesus was not an insurrectionist, his message was nonetheless subversive. The authority of human beings was limited, even if it was propped up by an interpretation of the scriptures. He exposed the hypocrisy of both religious and political leaders, and sought to overturn a system that labelled people as sinners, a permanent religious underclass. He clearly had major differences with the temple system of his day. His disruption of the money changers in the temple, described in violent terms, is one of the few episodes of his life that is contained in all four of the Gospels.[3]

Jesus is often thought of as an innocent victim, the sinless one who died for sinners, but William Stringfellow argues against this characterization:

Christ . . . is given over, and he surrenders, to Israel and Rome. And in the encounter with these powers there is exposed the relationship between Christ and all principalities and powers. The ecclesiastical and civil rulers who accuse, try, condemn, and execute Christ act not essentially for themselves as individuals, but as representatives—indeed, as servants—of the principalities. It is, of course, in the name of these powers that Christ is put on trial. He is accused of subverting and undermining the nation, of threatening the nation's existence, survival, and destiny. That this is the accusation should . . . dispose of the legend . . . that Christ is innocent of any offense and tried and condemned because of some corruption or failure or miscarriage of justice. Of the charges against him, Christ was guilty beyond doubt.[4]

Stringfellow's belief in Christ's guilt emphasizes that he was an actor in history, not an innocent, passive recipient of it. This active presence of "God's only Son, our Lord" leads to a way of hearing the Apostles' Creed as an active description of God's work throughout time, including the present. The creedal beliefs become more than descriptions. They become imperatives.

- ᚅ The belief that God created the world. This belief means that any indifference to the world falls short of God's desire for it. Creation matters now.

- ᚅ The belief that Jesus took on human flesh in its fullness and lived a human life raises human dignity and flourishing as among the highest of God's purposes. The Incarnation matters now.

ꚣ The belief that Jesus died and rose in the flesh to save humankind not solely for salvation in a heavenly future but also for liberation in the earthly present is the final revelation of God's "yes" to humankind. Salvation/Liberation matters now.

ꚣ The belief that the living and the dead in all times and all places form "the holy catholic church" and "the communion of saints," and that forgiveness of sins in this life is a preparation for the resurrection of the body and the life everlasting. Life in Communion/Community matters now.

Theological statements are not solely theoretical or philosophical. Theological traditions, including those central to Christian faith, are not frozen in time. They are reflections of human experience: past, present, and future. Thomas Merton wrote, "Tradition is the *renewal* in each generation and society, of the experiential knowledge of the mysteries of the faith."[5]

Such a renewal was led in the late nineteenth and early twentieth centuries by Anglicans like F.D. Maurice (1805–1872), Charles Gore (1853–1932), Vida Dutton Scudder (1861–1954), Emily Malbone Morgan (1862–1937), William Temple (1881–1944), R.H. Tawney (1880–1962), and Adelaide Teague Case (1887–1948).[6] For these men and women, the Incarnation was not a belief in a past event, but a manifesto for Christian action in the here and now. Maurice is universally thought to be the father of what came to be known as Christian Socialism.[7] In his theological writings he expressed the need for social ideals based on

Christian theology. He wrote in a time of rapid industrialization, and ever harsher living and working conditions for the poor. Economic theory and practice were being driven by such men as Adam Smith and John Stuart Mill, with their thought—and the world's economic life—increasingly dominated by self-interest rather than communal obligation.[8]

For Maurice, human beings were made to be inherently social. Philip Turner says of Maurice, "His focus on the social nature of human beings led him to say . . . that the watchword of the socialist is cooperation, and the watchword of an antisocial person is competition."[9] Maurice was adamant that we are *first* social beings, *then* individuals. It is, he said, the Incarnation that has established this truth, and baptism which brings it into existence and emphasizes its universality. The latter notion—universality—was essential for Maurice. He wrote in his seminal work *The Kingdom of Christ*:

> Christ came to establish a universal dispensation which did not exist previously . . . this dispensation is grounded upon a manifestation of God as absolute, universal love; upon the fact that [God] has entered into relations in the person of his Son with man as he is; and . . . to men so united to his Son, He gives his Spirit, that they may be endowed with that same universal love which is his own essential nature, and which has been displayed in the acts and sufferings of a real man. This revelation and this command lie at the foundation of the Christian Church; this is expressed in our Baptism "into the name of the Father, and of the Son, and of the Holy Ghost." They who enter this

state are bound to love their enemies, are bound to love all men, because they see that God loves all; they love those who hate and persecute them, because for those enemies and persecutors Christ died. They love even the enemies of God, because they regard them as creatures still bearing the flesh which Christ bore—not yet finally separated from Him, not deserted by his Spirit.[10]

Later, Charles Gore, bishop of Oxford, would write of the kenotic understanding of the Incarnation. This way of thinking was based in the ancient Christian hymn of Philippians 2, in which it is said, "[Christ] emptied himself, taking the form of a slave, being born in human likeness." "Emptied" is the Greek word ἐκένωσεν (ekenosen), from κενόω (kenow), "to empty." This self-emptying by the Son of his divine prerogatives meant two things to Gore: That there is a fundamental equality among human beings, and that the universal love so emphasized by Maurice is best expressed in service of others. This service is costly, and the church must be direct and clear about this cost. To be a Christian, Gore said, "is to be an intelligent participator in a corporate life consecrated to God." This corporate life includes concern for "the houses people live in, their wages, their social and commercial relations to one another, their amusements, the education they receive," etc. Christians live in "a commonwealth of mortal men with bodies as well as souls."[11] William Temple, archbishop of York and, briefly, of Canterbury, would go so far as to say, "The Church is the only society that exists for the benefit of those who are not its members."[12]

Simply put, the Incarnation expressed in the Apostles' Creed— "He was conceived by the power of the Holy Spirit and born of the

Virgin Mary"—has public and even political ramifications because by it God embraces the totality of human life, and the stance of this embrace is that of a servant. William Stringfellow says it nicely:

> The Incarnation means that God's passion for the world's actual life—including its politics, along with all else— is such that He enters and acts in this world for himself. . . . The Church and Christians are not simply involved in politics because of the nature of politics as such—by which all are involved and abstinence is a fiction—but because they honor and celebrate God's own action in this world, because they know that the world—in all its strife and confession, brokenness and travail—is the scene of God's work and the subject of God's love.[13]

Note in particular his aside: "By which all are involved and abstinence is a fiction." Non-involvement in social and political life is neither a choice for neutrality nor a declaration of independence from the fray. Non-involvement always sides with the status quo. For a Christian it is an abdication of her or his God-given participation in humanity, and, therefore, of God's work in the world. The Incarnation demands our participation, and so does the Crucifixion and Resurrection.

* * *

In reaction to something I said in a Palm Sunday Sermon, a parishioner took me aside and vigorously declared that the cross had nothing to do with politics. I replied that it was politics that got Jesus there. "OK, I'll give you that," he replied, "but I'm talking about the result—the result is eternal salvation. The cross is the way to heaven! Stick to the way to heaven, Father." This is a common sentiment. Yet if the cross (and the resurrection) are "the way to heaven," that way leads through the world. This truth is fundamental to our understanding of the Incarnation. God acted *in* the world *through* the flesh of Jesus Christ, including the experience of suffering and death.

What does the passion, death, and resurrection of Jesus have to do with public life? We cited above the place of Pontius Pilate and Jesus's arrest and trial under his political authority. Our time spent examining the Incarnation also reminds us: It was Jesus in human flesh who was crucified. Stringfellow sees Christ's crucifixion as the final act of God's bringing the whole creation—including what we often refer to as "the secular"—into the "province of the Gospel." He notes:

> The crucifixion is pre-eminently the event which brings all of the ordinary issues of existence in this world within the province of the gospel. There is no man, whatever his lot in life, beyond the outreach of the gospel or outside the range of the witness of the faithful. There is no nation or institution, nothing at all, whatever its characteristics or appearances, which is not a concern of the gospel and which is not the responsibility of the Body of Christ. The matters which occupy and preoccupy the daily attentions of secular existence are the issues which claim the attention of Christian faith. Concretely, that means that the people and the things with which an ordinary Christian comes into

contact from day to day are the primary and most profound issues of his faith and practice.[14]

Jesus speaks three times in John's Gospel about his "being lifted
up," by which the gospel writer tells us he means his crucifixion
(3:14, 8:28, 12:32). The final time he adds the phrase: "And I,
when I am lifted up from the earth, will draw all people to myself."
The use of "all" seems quite deliberate here. The Greek word used
is *pantas*, a masculine form of the word, so it is usually translated
"all men" or "all people" (the word for "men" or "people" is not present in the sentence). Other early manuscripts, however, have the
word as *panta*, a neuter form which could refer to "all things." Jesus
will draw the whole world to himself. The notion is not outside
of the Gospel of John's understanding of Jesus's mission; "God so
loved *the world* that he gave his only-begotten Son" (John 3:16 and
following).

In his 1964 address to the General Convention of The Episcopal Church, Presiding Bishop Arthur Lichtenberger used this
latter verse to make an important point about the Christian's place
in the world.

For God so loved the world—*the world*—that he gave his
only begotten Son, Jesus Christ, that all who believe in him
should not perish but have everlasting life. "The world"
here means everything that goes on in our lives, around us,
and in the uttermost parts of the earth. We cannot keep
our Christian convictions in one pocket and our thoughts
and actions about business and politics and the social order
in another pocket quite apart.[15]

It is not surprising that if the crucifixion is central to a proper understanding of the Christian's relationship with the world, the resurrection becomes so as well. Again, I turn to Stringfellow.

> I am sure of the Resurrection. . . . It is no special posses-
> sion or knowledge of my own, but it is the very event in
> which my own solidarity with every other man is consti-
> tuted. It is that unequivocal assurance that I am loved by
> One who loves all others which enables me to love myself
> and frees me to love another, any other, every other.[16]

At the end of the Apostles' Creed, in a litany of the man-ifestations of the Holy Spirit, we find the phrases, "the holy catholic church" and "the communion of saints." Both are social and spiritual in nature. They point to a future hope, but also a present reality in formation. "Catholic" is derived from the Greek *katholikos*, meaning "universal." It is another example of the church's use of a term that in the Greek of the time was unrelated to the spiritual realm. It gradually came to mean the church "in all places," and eventually also "in all times." To say the church is "holy" is not to say that it is focused on the other-worldly. Holiness is first of all a gift from God. The church does not make itself holy. The church—and its members—are holy because God is holy.[17]

Neither does holiness mean the church is somehow separate from the world. The church's holiness is set in the midst of the world. If holiness often implies a "setting apart," in biblical terms it also means "set in the midst of." We are meant to join with God in making a *katholikos,* a whole and undivided body that is itself set apart for making things whole in the world. This too is what Christians mean when they use the word "salvation."

Salvation is an ongoing process that is not only done to us, but by us. We are agents of salvation and liberation for the world, and not for the sole purpose of getting people into heaven. Again, Jesus taught us to pray, "Your kingdom come, your will be done, on earth as it is in heaven." The church has not always understood this truth. Oliver Wendell Holmes famously said, "Some people are so heavenly minded they are no earthly good."

The same dynamic exists in the phrase "communion of saints," which in Greek is the communion of the *hagioi*, "the holy ones." This does not refer to those remembered or rewarded for special deeds, exemplars of Christian living. "The holy ones" are the common people of God who, like the church itself, are made holy by God, who seek through their baptism to live lives of holiness in the world. In both instances, holiness is not a path to get out of the world, but a way of living in it. As we saw earlier, the Acts of the Apostles reports that Christians were first known as "The Way." They also came to be known as those who troubled others as "[those] people who have been turning the world upside down" (Acts 17:6). Clearly "The Way" had serious public and, therefore, social and political ramifications.

In the Baptismal Covenant of the Book of Common Prayer, the Apostles' Creed does not stand alone. It is followed by five questions which pertain to how baptismal faith is lived out in the world. Some have said the Apostles' Creed represents "orthodoxy" (literally "right praise," but used to mean "right theology") and the questions "orthopraxis" ("right practice"). On a surface level this is true, but as I have shown, the end of the Creed begs the question of practice with its talk of "the holy catholic church" and "the communion of saints."

The social and political implications of the Apostles' Creed end up being extensive. God is not passive in history, nor are we to be. Jesus's life, passion, death, and resurrection were moments in time with eternal—and, yes, historical—consequences. The Church has an active role to play in shaping the present and future. Why else describe it as "catholic," universal? No one, and no thing, is outside the reach of Christ's compassion and love. The same is true of his Body on earth. As my priest wisely said, "Every Christian's life is a fifth gospel." One might add that the church, the Way, is always writing subsequent chapters of the Acts of the Apostles.

Let us continue to explore how this faith turns the world upside down. How does it lead to an answer to the question of the nature of human dignity?

The Way of Dignity: A Way of Good News

> *Christianity is not the acceptance of a creed but the entrance into a life, and in that sacramental life timid distrust of high possibilities has no place.*
>
> —Vida Dutton Scudder,
> *Social Teachings of the Church Year*

Y ou must bring them to repentance."

In 2002 I was in Uganda, serving in my role as President of Integrity, visiting our first African chapter. Integrity was the fellowship and advocacy group of and for LGBTQ+ people in The Episcopal Church. It was founded in 1975 by Dr. Louie Crew. I served as its president from 1998 to 2003. The priest who worked to form the Ugandan group had scheduled a retreat day for the members with me as the leader. As the two of us planned the gathering, he was adamant about just one goal for the day—repentance. I asked him to explain why he thought this was so important. He replied, "If we are to have any chance at acceptance by the church here, they must demonstrate their commitment to sexual purity." He was certain that some of the group engaged in promiscuity.

Given the stance of the Anglican Church of Uganda against the slightest bit of acceptance of LGBTQ+ people in the church, I was fairly certain that no amount of repentance from sexual sin was going to change that attitude. I wondered aloud to my friend if there was something for the group members to struggle with that needed to happen *before* repentance: their own worth and dignity in the eyes of God. He remained skeptical, but gave me the opportunity to give it a try. For the retreat, I taught using John 15:12–16a and 1 John 4:16b–19.

> This is my commandment, that you love one another as I have loved you. No one has greater love than this, to lay down one's life for one's friends. You are my friends if you do what I command you. I do not call you servants any longer, because the servant does not know what the master is doing; but I have called you friends because I have made known to you everything that I have heard from my Father. You did not choose me but I chose you.

> God is love, and those who abide in love abide in God, and God abides in them. Love has been perfected among us in this: that we may have boldness on the day of judgment, because as he is, so are we in this world. There is no fear in love, but perfect love casts out fear; for fear has to do with punishment, and whoever fears has not reached perfection in love. We love because he first loved us.

I also taught the group members a hymn, the first verse of which is

I come with joy to meet my Lord,
forgiven, loved, and free,
in awe and wonder to recall
his life laid down for me.[1]

Twelve members of the group gathered that day. As I shared these texts, I was uncertain how they were being received. The students were attentive, that was obvious, but I could not read their faces clearly across cultural barriers. But I pressed my point. God loves you, the you that is right now, no matter what you have or have not done, and no matter what anyone else says about you. God always loves us first.

The group was quiet. When I asked them what their reaction was to these words there was silence for quite a long time. I waited. Finally, a middle-aged woman said, "I have been in church almost every Sunday of my life and I have never heard these words. How can they be true?" A young man said, "But we must do what God commands. God is our judge."

"Yes," I said, "both those things are true. But what does Jesus command us? To love each other. And who is the God who judges us? John says our judge, God, is love. And God's love comes before God's judgment." The young man, tears in his eyes, said, "I never knew this. I never knew this."

The responses from the group humbled me and reminded me of my own long experience of trying to earn God's grace, to be worthy of God's love. This tendency to put works before grace runs deep in most of us, because it is how the world works. I realized that it was even behind the pride I was feeling for having "gotten through" to the retreatants. Yet God loves us as God made us. We have dignity as children of God that no one can take away from us. In my experience, when I am sure of my own worth and yours, it is much easier to do the right thing. That I don't always do the right thing, that I make a mess of the gift God has given me, that then becomes a matter for repentance.

One of the young men at that retreat is now the pastor of the first Metropolitan Community Church in Uganda, a thriving community of acceptance which understands its mission to be the love of God for all humankind in the world. They take great risk meeting together, but are committed to act on behalf of the marginalized, and empower the marginalized to act on behalf of God.[2]

* * *

Some say "dignity" is difficult to define, or that it is not a theologically helpful word. The previously mentioned Christian Socialist movement of the late nineteenth and early twentieth century brought the word into common use in theological circles, associating it with equality and basic human rights. Philip Turner, in his book *Christian Socialism*, criticizes this use of the word. After examining several critiques of the term "dignity," he comes to the conclusion that "at best [dignity] has an unstable meaning whose imprecision serves as much to generate argument about the extent of its meaning as it does to establish a firm foundation for universal human rights."[3]

Admittedly, the English word "dignity" does not appear often in Bible translations. In the *New Revised Standard Version*, the word occurs only five times: four in the Old Testament and only once in the New Testament (1 Timothy 2:2). This lends to the argument that it is not a helpful theological word. The *King James Version*, however, gives us a clue as to what its theological content might be. The *King James Version* uses the word "dignities" twice (2 Peter 2:10 and Jude 8). The Greek word used in these two places is *doxa*, which is usually translated "glory," "honor," or "praise." "Glory" is most certainly a theological word. Its reference is normally to the divine, but it can also be ascribed to human beings. This is especially true in Paul's letters.

We boast in our hope of sharing the glory of God. (Romans 5:2)

And all of us, with unveiled faces, seeing the glory of the Lord as though reflected in a mirror, are being transformed into the same image from one degree of glory to another. (2 Cor. 3:18)

The glory of this mystery, which is Christ in you, the hope of glory. (Colossians 1:27)

Another term related to "dignity" is "worth" or "worthy." Like "glory," this is a term with biblical and theological gravitas. The Greek is *axios*, which forms a portion of the contemporary Greek word for "dignity," *axioprepeia*. The English word "worth" also appears in the word "worship," originally "worthship," the acknowledgement of the worth of another. In worship we give ultimate worth to God, but it is an essential aspect of Christian worship that this dynamic works both ways. In worship we give worth to God, and God gives worth to us.

This examination of the word "dignity" is necessary because of its use in the Baptismal Covenant of the Book of Common Prayer. The action questions that are the second half of this covenant not only use the term "dignity," but place it at the very end: *Will you strive for justice and peace among all people, and respect the dignity of every human being?* It serves as the cymbal crash at the end of the crescendo that is built through the five questions. I submit that the phrase at the beginning of the questions—*continue in the apostles' teaching and fellowship*—and its final phrase—*respect the dignity of every human person*—form an inclusio, encapsulating the way of life the covenant demands of us. This inclusio could be expressed in this way: Will you bring the past experience of the followers of Jesus into the present as you act to build God's dream for the future, the fundamental building block being the gift of human dignity?

I take Turner's point that the term "dignity" can be slippery, but I do not think this is true in the context of the Baptismal Covenant, where human dignity is clearly understood to be a gift from God, a gift we are called both to acknowledge and support in one another. This dignity does rest in human equality, but also, as the last question of the covenant implies, is dependent on the presence of justice and peace. I also believe there is more at stake here than human rights. What is at stake is the very gospel the followers of Jesus are to *proclaim by word and example*, a phrase from the third of the five covenantal questions. Let's take the questions now in turn.

> *Will you continue in the apostles' teaching and fellowship,*
> *in the breaking of bread and in the prayers?*

The first praxis question of the covenant is a direct quote from the Acts of the Apostles. It is one of a handful of summary statements made in Acts about the early Christian community. The full description at the end of Acts 2 is:

They devoted themselves to the apostles' teaching and fellowship, to the breaking of bread and the prayers. Awe came upon everyone, because many wonders and signs were being done by the apostles. All who believed were together and had all things in common; they would sell their possessions and goods and distribute the proceeds to all, as any had need. Day by day, as they spent much time together in the temple, they broke bread at home and ate their food with glad and generous hearts, praising God and having the goodwill of all the people. And day by day the Lord added to their number those who were being saved. (Acts 2:42–47)

Another description closes Acts 4, with similar sentiments:

Now the whole group of those who believed were of one heart and soul, and no one claimed private ownership of any possessions, but everything they owned was held in common. With great power the apostles gave their testimony to the resurrection of the Lord Jesus, and great grace was upon them all. There was not a needy person among them, for as many as owned lands or houses sold them and brought the proceeds of what was sold. They laid it at the apostles' feet, and it was distributed to each as any had need. (Acts 4:32–35)

Commentators frequently use words such as "idyllic" and "idealized" in discussing these passages. Whether or not that is true, they must have had some basis in reality, and they certainly are attempts by Luke—the writer of Acts—to establish a baseline description of the dynamics of early Christian community. The *koinonia* (fellowship) of these first believers was a living out of Jesus's teaching, particularly about life in the kingdom of God. This is how God's kingdom comes, as Jesus taught his followers to pray (Luke 11:3).[4]

Commentator Luke Timothy Johnson shows that the four fundamentals stated in Acts 2:42 (apostles' teaching, fellowship, breaking of bread, prayers) are elaborated in 2:43–47.[5]

Acts 2:42	Acts 2:43–47
Apostles' teaching	Wonders & signs that create awe/fear
Fellowship	Sharing possessions
Breaking of bread	Meals shared in homes
The prayers	Attendance in the temple praising God

This arrangement shows us that the descriptions in Acts 2 and 4 are real world, here and now, descriptions of Christian living. They may have been ideals whose practice was inconsistent, but ideals for which to strive were a significant part of Jesus's teaching. They were, as well, distinctive, both in terms of Jewish and Greek/Roman culture. The sharing of possessions, for instance, is not an Old Testament ideal. Even the practice of Jubilee only returned such things as land and debt to their original distribution.[6] There was no explicit goal of equal possessions. Greek/Roman religious culture was built on sacrifice to capricious gods, not the ideal of common worship with what later would be called "the sacrifice of praise and thanksgiving."

The sharing of possessions or "holding all things in common" described in Acts has long vexed Christians. Is Luke proposing communism? Two things must be said about this question. First of all, it is never helpful to project later or contemporary ideologies onto biblical texts. The result is always mischief. Second, the text *is* ideal, but also has its roots in practice. It cannot, therefore, be ignored or dismissed with the wave of a we-know-better hand.

Perhaps it is helpful to set aside the meaning of "possessions," and focus on the more fundamental notion of equality, and, especially, what William Temple called equality of status, which he understood to have economic (and therefore political) implications.

> If all are children of one Father, then all are equal heirs of a status in comparison with which the apparent differences of quality and capacity are unimportant; in the deepest and most important of all—their relationship to God—all are equal. Why should some of God's children have full opportunity to develop their capacities in freely-chosen occupations, while others are confined to a stunted form of existence, enslaved to types of labour which represent no personal choice but the sole opportunity offered? The Christian cannot ignore a challenge in the name of justice. He must either refuse it or, accepting it, devote himself to the removal of the stigma.[7]

Is this kind of equality—one with earthly content as well as spiritual—part of the "apostles' teaching and fellowship"? We must say "yes" based on several pieces of evidence. First is the phrase "apostles' teaching and fellowship" itself. Not enough is said about the importance of this pairing. They are inseparable: Teaching without fellowship is an intellectual exercise, dry and not altogether compelling. Fellowship without teaching leaves the human being at his own wits end. It turns the church into just another social club. Together "teaching and fellowship" is a lively thing; to use church words we would say they are the twin pillars of orthodoxy (right praise or belief) and orthopraxis (right action). If nothing else, the structure of the Baptismal Covenant in the Book of Common Prayer indicates the essential nature of both in the Christian life.

Another witness to the equality proclaimed by the early church is Quadratus's proclamation in his "Letter to Diognetus: The Mystery of a New People," which tells us much of what we know of early Christian life beyond the New Testament. This "New People" is formed in baptism and nourished in the Eucharist, which is the enactment of the "Mystery" itself. The New People are fundamentally equal. The roots of this equality are found in the words of Paul: "There is no longer Jew or Greek, there is no longer slave or free, there is no longer male or female; for all of you are one in Christ Jesus" (Galatians 3:27–28).[8] The practice of this equality in the Eucharist is emphasized by Paul in his chastisement of the Corinthian believers, whose coming together was fraught with social distinctions, so much so that he declares their coming together "not really to eat the Lord's Supper" (1 Cor. 11:17–22).

This opening question of the Covenant is about worship. Worship is where Christians are formed and re-formed a new people by the power of the Holy Spirit. This occurs both in what some people call "spirit-filled" worship and in the quietest and most sedate settings. The Holy Spirit's presence is guaranteed. Episcopal Theologian John Booty writes,

The Holy Spirit is always active in the holy community, liberating us from the need to agonize over where the Spirit is or should be. The Spirit is present among us in our worship of God. Public worship—public spirituality—frees us from individualistic preoccupation and from passing fancies and foolishness.[9]

What matters is not our ability to call upon the Spirit, but our participation in the Spirit's gracious outpouring. "Participation" seems a mundane word, but it was a central concept of Anglicanism's seminal theologian, Richard Hooker. Booty summarizes Hooker's spirituality of participation in this way:

The spirituality of participation is fundamentally social because the work of the Holy Spirit is social, restoring us to relationship with God and with one another, reconciling relationships in families, in work places, in the political and economic arenas, in international affairs and in the church. The social dimensions of spirituality stand over against all our likes and dislikes, all racial and ethnic divisions; likewise, they sit in constant judgment on our avarice, greed, arrogance, and pride.[10]

In worship we participate in Christ and Christ participates in us. But this mutuality is not a closed loop, as we are called to participate in the world with open hearts and to allow the world to participate in us. The Eucharist is our pattern for life in and for the world. Beyond our individual participation, the Eucharist participates in the world and the world participates in the Eucharist. As William Stringfellow says,

> To celebrate the Word of God in the sacramental worship
> of a congregation is an anticipation of the discernment of
> the same Word of God in the common life of the world.
> To be in the presence of the Word of God while in the
> world authenticates the practice of sacramental life within
> the congregation. One confirms and is confirmed by the
> other. . . . It is this experience . . . this interpenetra-
> tion of his secular and religious lives which identifies the
> Christian.[11]

Worship may provide respite from the world, but it also propels us back into it. This dual function is an absolute necessity, about which the Hebrew prophets are clear. Amos proclaims on behalf of God: "I hate, I despise your festivals, and I take no delight in your solemn assemblies. . . . But let justice roll down like waters, and righteousness like an ever-flowing stream" (Amos 5:21–24). There is a similar sentiment in Isaiah 58: "Is this not the fast that I choose: to loose the bonds of injustice . . . to let the oppressed go free, and to break every yoke?" This understanding of fasting and worship leads to action in the world: "You shall be called repairer of the breach, the restorer of streets to live in." Both of these passages lead to a fundamental understanding of worship: Worship without the practice of holiness and justice is so much "noise." It is at best self-indulgent and at worst a denial of God's purposes.

Will you persist in resisting evil, and, whenever you fall into sin,
repent and return to the Lord?

The baptismal rite begins with a renunciation of evil and sin, but the prayer book understands this renunciation as a beginning, not an ending. It is something that must be repeated again and again. The presence of evil and sin in the world and in the human heart requires both lifelong resistance and lifelong persistence.

The primary virtue called for here is that of honesty—honesty about oneself and honesty about the world. It requires the practice of "discernment," which Walter Wink defines as "the gift of seeing reality as it really is."[12] True honesty about ourselves opens us up to the spiritual reality so that, as New Testament Scholar William Countrymann says, "I can see those who have harmed me as more like myself than different and that I am prepared to build a future with them."[13] This is not an easy way of life. It never has been, and Christians have chafed under its yoke almost from the beginning. If anything, in our current world, it is more difficult than it has ever been because of the polarizations that structure so much of our public reality, particularly our political reality.

There's a word that underlies this question of sin and repentance that isn't used in the question. That word is forgiveness. If honesty is an assumed virtue in this question, so is forgiveness. Indeed, forgiveness is the only way we can live in honesty. It is inevitable that when we speak honestly, we will speak in disagreement with one another. To disagree, and even to argue out our disagreements, is part of being human. The Bible testifies to the reality—nay, the importance—of even arguing with God. Abraham does it (Genesis 18); Moses does it (Exodus 32); Job does it (chapter 13). The Psalms are full of it (see, for example,

Psalm 44). At the beginning of the Book of Isaiah, God asks for an argument.

> Wash yourselves; make yourselves clean; remove the evil of your doings from before my eyes; cease to do evil, learn to do good; seek justice, rescue the oppressed, defend the orphan, plead for the widow. Come now, let us argue it out, says the Lord: though your sins are like scarlet, they shall be like snow; though they are red like crimson, they shall become like wool. (Isa. 1:16–18)

What is critically important here is that the argument is a way back into relationship with God. "Make your case," God seems to say. And before the case is made comes the proclamation, "I am ready to forgive," that is, "I am ready to renew our relationship."

Repentance is the desire and willingness to renew a relationship that is strained or broken. It is a fundamental part of the baptismal way of life, the way of reconciliation. No one claims repairing broken relationships is easy. In fact, it is hard work, perhaps even counter-cultural. Reconciliation eschews rivalry, the win-lose paradigm that is a powerful part of our culture. Choosing to repair relationships—seek reconciliation—is the road less traveled among us.

Perhaps the chief problem standing in the way of reconciliation is the question of justice. That is the difficulty I most hear when I teach or preach on these themes. Is nothing simply wrong? If everything is right, don't we descend into chaos? These questions are as old as the Bible. Paul wrestles with them in Romans 6, asking, "Should we continue in sin in order that grace may abound?" His answer, shouted in 6:1–2, is a resounding "By no means!"

William Countrymann tackles this "by no means," meditating on grace and forgiveness:

> Forgiveness . . . is much misunderstood. Forgiveness is not a pretense, a fabrication, a lie about the past. It does not say, "Oh, that never happened," or "Everything is just as it was before." Forgiveness always begins by admitting the facts of the matter wherever there has been harm and hurt and wrongdoing. Forgiveness does not mean telling lies about humanity, either—pretending that everyone is always straightforward, honest, kind, or good. Forgiveness isn't risk-free, of course, but it doesn't mean taking stupid and unnecessary risks with people who have shown themselves vicious or violent. It doesn't mean refusing to learn from the past or to take reasonable precautions.[14]

The baptismal promise to repent and return to God when we sin, is a promise always to seek relationship, first with God, then with others, including ourselves, because in the end the hardest person for anyone to forgive is often themself.

There is a great fear in our public life to admit that one has been wrong or to profess a change of heart. Retaining one's good standing with social and political allies and what is often called one's "base," is, in practice, the highest virtue for many. This frequently means holding in contempt those with whom one disagrees, to the point of questioning their good will, patriotism, and even humanity. The politics of dehumanizing the other is a major stumbling block to the social project of working for the common good and dignity of all.

Once again, what seems to be a highly personal question—to recognize sin, repent, and turn back to God—is actually a major building block in the great spiritual and social enterprise of building the kingdom of God "on earth as it is in heaven." Vida Scudder, an Episcopal educator and witness for peace in the first half of the twentieth century, speaks of Lent (the time of the church year most given to repentance) as having definite social implications. She writes: "Personal lives can be purified by resolute abstinence and prayer, till they become instruments of social salvation. The disciplines [of fasting, prayer, and repentance] to which Lent calls us are no self-centered indulgence in the quest for private holiness; . . . they are a preparation for citizenship."[15]

One of the most important aspects of the Christian commitment to repentance and forgiveness is the belief that we are not in competition with one another either on the spiritual plane or the secular one. A key part of the dream of God for the world and for humankind is that we give up our obsession with rivalry as a way of life. This is behind a vital proclamation of the early church: the God who shows no partiality. After his encounter with the Gentile Cornelius and his household in Acts 10, Peter begins his reflection, "I truly understand that God shows no partiality." Paul proclaims the same in several of his letters, including in Romans 2, when he says quite simply, "For God shows no partiality."

God's lack of partiality is, perhaps, deceptively simple. Competition and rivalry are a natural human reaction to life. We easily slip into "group think," which almost inevitably leads to judgments of others as better or worse. In Romans, after Paul proclaims the God of "no partiality," he must come to terms with the major division in his world: Jew and Gentile. He uses the image of grafting the branch of a wild olive tree onto that of a cultivated olive tree in Romans 11, writing, "You [Gentiles] have been cut from what is by nature a wild olive tree and grafted, contrary to nature, into a cultivated olive tree." Paul is challenging both his Gentile and his Jewish readers to move beyond human notions of what is natural and unnatural, acceptable and unacceptable. He is saying both groups have to embrace the impartiality of God. The impartiality that is part of the nature of God must be chosen by humankind, a choice that is so difficult, it can seem "contrary to nature." Almost always, it requires our repentance, our willingness to turn around, to see differently, to love in a way we thought not possible.

The assumption of superiority by Western culture (with its racial, ethnic, and patriarchal components) and the obsessive need for particular cultures or nations to proclaim themselves as the "greatest," are realities the Christian must choose to act against, if we are to have any claim to be on the side of the impartial God.

*Will you proclaim by word and example
the good news of God in Christ?*

What is the good news? At the Lambeth Conference of 1998, the once-a-decade-or-so meeting of all the bishops of the various dioceses of the constituent member churches of the Anglican Communion, convened by the archbishop of Canterbury, I was present as an unofficial observer representing Integrity.[16] The place of LGBTQ+ persons in the Communion and the bishops' collective stance on homosexuality was a hot button issue that year. At an open presentation I said,

This conversation [about human sexuality] is about the Gospel and what we think and believe it is and how we practice it day by day. I have had several conversations these days that have followed on the question, "What do you want?" What I really want is a good long talk about the real question, the only question that matters. "What is the Gospel?" And yes, then, but only then, how does it relate to my sexuality and yours.[17]

That conference chose to reject "homosexual practice as incompatible with Scripture," while at the same time committing the bishops "to listen to the experience of homosexual people" and "condemn irrational fear of homosexuals."[18] It was a decision met with great sorrow and anger by LGBTQ+ people and their supporters throughout the world. Even the positive statement about listening and the condemnation of fear were met by extreme skepticism. Like most marginalized people, we know when scraps are being thrown from the table with no intention of giving us a seat.

That was twenty-five years ago, and, despite our skepticism, one can see in the long term that the question about the gospel was taken up with great sincerity by many, and, in The Episcopal Church as well as elsewhere in the Communion, to great effect. It was not the sudden realization of an entirely new thing, but a deepening understanding of the purposes of God "on earth as it is in heaven." The understanding is an ongoing process; the struggle continues, but the point here is that the Good News is not solely the proclamation of salvation that ends in eternal life. No, Christian people have a mission on earth. As Edward Schillebeeckx puts it,

Christians are called to bear witness to Jesus Christ and thus to spread the gospel, because they want to further God's kingdom of justice and love throughout the world. . . . the correct approach of true mission is to make people aware of the unacceptable character of the oppression under which they live. . . . The gospel is shown to men and women by its liberating fruit.[19]

Liberation—freedom—is at the heart of the gospel because the free God is at the heart of the gospel as well as the fundamental belief that human beings are made in the image of God. If made in the image of God, then humankind is free for abundant life. Jesus said, "I came that they may have life, and have it abundantly" (John 10:10). Everyone is free to live abundant lives, or no one is. As Jesus also says, "And I, when I am lifted up, will draw all people to myself" (John 12:32).

For many African slaves in the United States, the gospel meant singing of their liberation even under the oppressive yoke of white men and women. If God was free, then they were created to be free. When their songs included the expectation of home, the masters heard a happy hope of heaven, but the enslaved people were singing about the home of freedom. Their song of Good News carries on, long after chattel slavery has ended.[20] For women, the gospel means the right to flourish as human beings made in the image of God.[21] For LGBTQ+ persons, the gospel means that the promise made to them of having "a full and equal claim on the love, acceptance, and pastoral care of the church" will be fulfilled, and the love in their relationships will be experienced by all as a reflection of the love of God for the world.[22]

Criticism has been levelled at this understanding of the gospel, claiming that it is self-centered, a gospel of "my rights," rather than a proclamation of salvation found in Christ. It must be admitted that is a danger, although the notion that the gospel is primarily about salvation from sin and entrance into heaven is open to the same dangers. Selfishness is a strong enough impulse for all human beings. We can take anything and turn it into something primarily about ourselves or about some idol to which we give our primary allegiance. Human rights can become an idol. So can freedom. So can eternal salvation. So can the sacraments.

In her book, *The Dangers of Christian Practice*, Lauren Winner makes the important point that all Christian practices can be "damaged." She does not mean by this simply that they are subject to misuse (although they are). She means that in their *faithful* doing they can undermine themselves from within. "Because nothing created is untouched by the Fall," she writes, "Christians should not be surprised when lovely and good, potentially gracious Christian gestures are damaged, or when human beings deploy those Christian gestures in the perpetuation of damage."[23]

For example, Winner sees in baptism a dichotomy that must be held in balance and often is not. Baptism both separates a person from the world into a heavenly community (a community which has a greater claim on the baptized person than any earthly community such as the nuclear family) *and* celebrates their uniqueness as a gift from God to be used in and for the world. The latter, in particular, is often overtaken by the celebration of the gift of a child to a particular family. This frequently overtakes the sense of separation when its proper function is to balance it.[24] Baptism is a celebration of the gift of an individual *and* the destiny of the individual as a part of the Body of Christ.

Winner's observations are important to consider when dealing with the criticism that the gospel articulated in baptism has become a selfish expression of an individual's human rights. Such a claim expresses an unbalanced understanding of baptism. Baptism *is* about rights (as they flow naturally from a commitment to human dignity) *and* it is about responsibilities beyond the self, having been ingrafted into the household of God. The self is empowered with ultimate dignity in baptism *and* called to the sacrificial life of service. As William Stringfellow says,

> The Christian is suspicious of respectability and moderation and success and popularity. And this is so because the genius of the Christian life, both for a person and for the company of Christians, is the freedom constantly to be engaged in giving up its own life in order to give the world new life.[25]

Stringfellow's words may seem to lean too strongly in the direction of the responsibilities of the baptismal life. Yet what he does here is help us understand just what is meant by the human dignity that constitutes so much of the Good News. He makes clear what dignity is not: "respectability and moderation and success and popularity." Dignity is rather freedom, the freedom out of one's own sense of self in relationship to God and the community of faith that can choose the life of service in and for the world. This brings us to the final questions of the Baptismal Covenant. What does this life of service look like?

CHAPTER 7

The Way of Dignity: A Way of Reconciliation

To work for reconciliation is to want to realize God's dream for humanity—when we will know that we are indeed members of one family, bound together in a delicate network of interdependence.

—Desmond Tutu, *No Future Without Forgiveness*

Will you seek and serve Christ in all persons,
loving your neighbor as yourself?

In order to fully understand the implications of the final questions of the Baptismal Covenant, one must first seek to answer: Who is my neighbor?

In the Gospel of Luke, a lawyer's question to Jesus—And who is my neighbor?—led not to a pronouncement but a story, known popularly as "The Parable of the Good Samaritan" (Luke 10:25–37). The lawyer knows the pronouncement, or the "summary of the law," as it is often called: "You shall love the Lord your God with all your heart, and with all your soul, and with all your strength, and with all your mind; and your neighbor as yourself." This pronouncement, a combination of Deuteronomy 6:5 and Leviticus 19:18, had been taught by many Jewish teachers before Jesus.[1]

Luke tells us that the lawyer asked the question "wanting to justify himself," probably meaning he wanted his own biases to be confirmed. Those prejudices certainly included a disdain for Samaritans, whom the Jews of Jesus's day considered heretics and, therefore, unclean.[2] Thus Jesus's choice of a Samaritan as the hero of the story, the one who acted as a neighbor, would have made a significant impact, although we are not told of the lawyer's reaction, only Jesus's injunction to "Go and do likewise."

The lawyer's question, however, reverberates through the centuries as the Christian community grapples with issues of who is in and who is out, and how the outsider is to be treated. To say the church failed more often than not to "go and do likewise" is a vast understatement. The struggle continues to our own day. Yet it can be argued that this summary of the law, paired with "the golden rule" of doing to others as you would have them do to you, is at the very heart of Jesus's teaching. St. Paul summarizes the teaching even further in Galatians 5:14: "For the *whole law* is summed up in a single commandment: "You shall love your neighbor as yourself." The writer of the Epistle of James goes so far as to call love of neighbor "the royal law" (James 2:8).

Dorothy Day, one of the founders of the Catholic Worker movement, told this story, reflecting on just how difficult following this "royal law" can be:

One priest had his catechism classes write us questions as to our work after they had the assignment . . . to read my book The Long Loneliness. The majority of them asked the same question: "How can you see Christ in people?" And we only say: it is an act of faith, constantly repeated.

It is an act of hope, that we can awaken these same acts in their hearts with the help of God, and the Works of Mercy. . . . The mystery of the poor is this: That they are Jesus, and what you do for them you do for him. It is the only way we have of knowing and believing in our love.[3]

The fourth question of the Baptismal Covenant includes a call not just to love of neighbor as oneself, but also to seek and serve Christ in all people. This is a reference to Matthew 25:31–46, often referred to as "The Parable of the Sheep and the Goats." In this judgment scene, the criterion for assessment is love of neighbor on a practical level: The enthroned Son of Man gathers the nations and divides people into sheep and goats. The sheep are judged as blessed, because "I was hungry and you gave me food, I was thirsty and you gave me something to drink, I was a stranger and you welcomed me, I was naked and you gave me clothing, I was sick and you took care of me, I was in prison and you visited me." The goats are cursed because they did not do these things. Those being judged do not know when they saw the Son of Man in any of these conditions. The judge's answer: "Just as you did it to one of the least of these who are members of my family, you did (or did not do) it to me."[4]

The first and most fundamental point here is that we do not get to decide who is our neighbor. This applies whether we are acting as a neighbor, or being acted upon by a neighbor. How this applies to our political and social life may seem obvious, but it is also staggeringly subversive to our tendency to form groups, apply labels, see differences before we see similarities, and act with prejudice. "Take care of your own before you take care of others" and "first take care of number one" are popular notions that are, simply put, antithetical to the gospel (and found nowhere in the Bible). "Others" are people with whom we are called into relationships of equality and for whom we have responsibility. These truths lie at the heart of what it means to be Christian.

Former Archbishop of Canterbury Rowan Williams famously said that "baptism catches us up into solidarities not of our own choosing." These solidarities are with all those whom Jesus has taught us to call neighbors. As Williams implies, the unity to which we are called in the baptismal way of living can be uncomfortable, because solidarity does not include agreement or indeed likeness in any way. It is a universal solidarity, not even confined to other Christians. In quoting Williams's statement about solidarity, former Presiding Bishop Frank Griswold said that when we renew our baptismal vows, "We make clear to one another and to the world . . . that being bound together in Christ through baptism transcends all our differences."[5]

It is vitally important to understand that transcending our differences does not mean obliterating them. Following Jesus does not mean adopting a uniformity of thought, conviction, or experience. As Richard Hooker articulated clearly in the sixteenth century:

> God hath created nothing simply for itself: but each thing in all things, and of every thing each part in the other hath such interest, that in the whole world nothing is found whereunto any thing created can say, "I need thee not."[6]

The language Hooker uses is interesting: "every thing" and "any thing." His vision of solidarity—the need all things have for

every thing—is not limited to human beings. We need to understand that our affirmative answer to this question of seeking Christ
and loving the neighbor includes our regard, stewardship, and love
of the whole of creation. Some have suggested that the questions
of the Baptismal Covenant lack a commitment to the care of creation, a commitment so very important in our time of climate
crisis. The call to care for the earth and all its creatures is there,
however, in an expansive understanding of the presence of Christ
in the whole of creation and the neighbor found in all things.

What does it mean to say, "I need you," to every person created by God and to every element of God's creation? It means a
commitment to reconciliation as our highest purpose. The Book of
Common Prayer teaches that reconciliation is at the heart of every
Christian's ministry: "to carry on Christ's work of reconciliation
in the world." This ministry is part of the mission of the church,
which is "to restore all people to unity with God and each other
in Christ." Again, unity is not uniformity. Unity is the knowledge
and conviction that I can say of no one or no thing (in Hooker's
words), "I need thee not." To be reconciled is to be committed to
a relationship with another despite our differences, a commitment
that includes proclaiming the gospel and promoting justice, peace,
and love.[7]

Reconciliation is no easy task because it is by nature radical,
that is, going to the root of our responsibility for the common
good. Reaching Hooker's vision of the reciprocity of human and
creaturely need is often just the beginning. From this insight of
fundamental equality must come the real struggle for just relationships and "the restoration of justice, equity, and dignity."[8] Too often
reconciliation is individualized, and its goal thought to be you and

me forgiving one another for past wrongs. Again, that is a step. But further—and more difficult—work is required. What caused the breach? How can that breach be restored? This radical step is often where the work of reconciliation gets hung up, because we often must face systemic issues that are not solved by any one individual's action, but require communal effort.

Reconciliation is often corporate in nature. The rich, for instance, cannot reconcile with the poor simply by saying, "I'm sorry for the conditions under which you live, let me lend you a hand." To pursue true reconciliation, we are called to ask: What do we need to do so that the rich do not need to lend a hand any longer? What needs to change systemically so that the poor can participate fully in human flourishing? Or, as Verna Dozier framed the question at the heart of reconciliation ministry: "What are the systems and structures that will give dignity to all people? How can we bring those systems into being?"[9]

Talk of reconciliation also means struggling not only with the question of who or what is called "neighbor," but also with the question of who or what is "enemy." Jesus was unequivocal about our relationships with our enemies. "You have heard it said," he taught the crowd gathered on a hillside in Galilee, "'You shall love your neighbor and hate your enemy.' But I say to you, Love your enemies and pray for those who persecute you" (Matthew 5:43–44). This is an astounding proclamation all by itself, but the reasons Jesus gives for this pronouncement intensify his teaching.

So that you may be children of your Father in heaven; for he makes his sun to rise on the evil and on the good, and sends rain on the righteous and on the unrighteous. For if you love those who love you, what reward do you have? Do not even the tax collectors do the same? And if you greet only your brothers and sisters, what more are you doing than others? Be perfect, therefore, as your heavenly Father is perfect. (Matt 5:45–48)

It is important to know that there is no direct commandment in the Hebrew Scriptures to "hate your enemies." "Love your neighbors," as we have seen, comes from Leviticus 19:18. When Jesus begins with "you have heard it said," he is no doubt speaking of common wisdom from the time. Of course, one hates one's enemies. That is among the most natural of human tendencies, and it does fit into the worldview of much of the wisdom literature[10] of the Hebrew Scriptures, perhaps best summarized by Psalm 1, which ends, "For the LORD watches over the righteous, but the way of the wicked will perish." Wisdom literature tends to divide the world into good and bad, righteous and unrighteous. Yet Jesus pushed against this easy dualism. It is not, he said, how God operates in the world.

Politics throughout history has tended toward this dualism, at times more extreme than others. Most observers would agree that at this moment in the United States, dualism reigns.[11] The categories are clear: good and bad, patriotic and unpatriotic, lovers and haters of freedom, capitalists and socialists. It can be argued that this dualistic tendency is endemic to the way of life in the United States. The country was born in the dualism of those who favored independence and the Tories, who did not, of the indigenous people whose land this was and the European settlers who believed this land was their divine destiny, of the enslaved and the free. Those involved in the governance of the new country early on favored a two-party political system. They believed a competition of ideas would be healthy for the new nation. George Washington, who was elected president without affiliation with a political party, warned that the two-party system that was developing would lead to conflict and stagnation and leave the country open to despotism.[12]

The priority of love of neighbor on the part of Christians must always push against this dualism and factionalism. Both are antithetical to any Christian vision of political life. Love of the enemy, or even those who simply oppose any of our dearly held convictions, is actually an imperative for a present that works for all and a future which is aimed at the common good. There is "no other way to God for our time but through the enemy," says Walter Wink, "for loving the enemy has become the key to human survival in the nuclear age and to personal transformation." The enemy is a "gift," says Wink, "to see aspects of ourselves that we cannot discover any other way than through our enemies."[13]

Wink is talking about the work of reconciliation, bringing to it an important twist. The path of reconciliation is not simply the path of changing another for the good. It is also the openness to self-transformation. If I am truly to be reconciled, I must recognize my own need to change. This is extraordinarily difficult work; it is, and always has been, and always will be. In a factionalized environment, seeking reconciliation or political compromise can be considered a heresy. It can even lead to persecution by those with whom we most identify (such as being labelled a RINO, that is, "Republican In Name Only"). Again, Christians of any political stripe, or group membership, or national citizenry must be ready to push against these tendencies. Factionalism must always be overcome by gospel values.

There's no better place to find warrant for this truth than the Letter to the Ephesians. Christ is portrayed here as the one who overcomes factionalism in any form.

> In Christ Jesus you who once were far off have been brought near by the blood of Christ. For he is our peace; in his flesh he has made both groups into one and has broken down the dividing wall, that is the hostility between us. He has abolished the law with its commandments and ordinances, that he might create in himself one new humanity in place of the two, thus making peace, and might reconcile both groups to God in one body through the cross, thus putting to death that hostility through it. (Eph. 3:13–16)

Paul is speaking directly to the conflict between Jews and Gentiles, but there is no reason to think this pattern of peacemaking is not a universal one. "The law with its commandments and ordinances" can refer to those political dogmas that become rigid markers of the righteous and the unrighteous, or those social and cultural boundaries that become hard and fast divisions between the welcome and the unwelcome. This is equally true of any side of any division, including political and religious ones. Richard Rohr says of this pattern in Ephesians: "It's the only truly transformative pattern in human history."[14]

What about the call to perfection in the passage from Matthew about loving enemies? It commands, "Be perfect, therefore, as your heavenly Father is perfect." Does not this mean that there is an unbending truth and absolute standard? Wink proposes that the Greek word translated "perfect" (*teleios*) does not mean perfect in any moral sense. *Teleios*, he says is not a moral term in Greek. It comes from the world of mathematics (in particular, geometry) and art.[15] The statement about perfection is taken from Deuteronomy 18:13, where in the Greek translation available to Matthew the word *teleios* translates the Hebrew word *tamim*. Yet *tamim* has the meaning of "whole, complete, finished." It also sometimes means "having integrity." Those are all very different concepts than "perfect." The Hebrew word certainly has less of a sense of exclusiveness.[16] All this may have come into play when Luke renders this same sentence in his gospel as, "Be merciful, just as your Father is merciful" (Luke 6:36).

I have spent much time with this particular question of the Baptismal Covenant because I believe it is so central to it and to the Christian faith as a whole. I also believe it can be the most important contribution Christians have to bring to political and social discourse. "Love your neighbor as yourself" is the measuring rod for Christian participation in the world. This is what we do if we do nothing else.

> *Will you strive for justice and peace among all people,*
> *and respect the dignity of every human being?*

The last question of the Baptismal Covenant brings us back to the query with which we began our discussion of the covenant in chapter 5: What is dignity?

To answer the question, let us begin with God. Christianity has always spoken of immanence as well as transcendence. But the immanence has tended to be focused completely on the one man, the incarnation of God, the fully God and fully human, Jesus. The Holy Spirit is occasionally understood to be part of this immanence, but the Church in the West has lacked a robust understanding of the work of the Holy Spirit. In the words of the Nicene Creed, the Holy Spirit's work "proceeds from the Father and the Son." The Eastern Church, however, has a clearer sense of the work of the Spirit, symbolized by their rejection of the formula "from the Father and the Son." The Nicene Creed of the East says that the Spirit simply "proceeds from the Father." The Spirit has an independent and equal life within the Holy Trinity, and, therefore, on earth among human beings.[17]

An emphasis on the transcendence of God serves to protect the mystery of God. Thomas Aquinas, the great pre-reformation Catholic theologian of the thirteenth century, put it in terms that are still clear after 800 years:

> Our mind is not proportionate to the divine substance, that which is the substance of God remains beyond our intellect and so is unknown to us. Hence the supreme knowledge which we have of God is to know that we do not know God, insofar as we know that God surpasses all that we can understand.[18]

Yet this is not all there is to say about God. Yes, God is Mystery, "unknowable" (although the better term may be "incomprehensible"), but, paradoxically, God seeks to be known. Our God is relational. Roman Catholic and feminist theologian Elizabeth Johnson makes clear this paradox and its importance.

The one relational God, precisely in being utterly transcendent, not limited by any finite category, is capable of
the most radical immanence, being intimately related to
everything that exists. And the effect of divine drawing
near and passing by [i.e., God's immanence] is always to
empower creatures toward life and well-being in the teeth
of the antagonistic structure of reality.[19]

God is relational both within the Trinity and without. The
relation, or communion, within the Trinity is often spoken of using
the Greek word *perichoresis*, meaning "to lead around" or "dance."
This dance, however, does not remain within the Trinity, but spills
out into the world, with which God also desires communion,
a reciprocal relationship. Johnson has a wonderful image in that
God is always "approaching from the future to attract [the world]
toward *shalom*"[20] (the Hebrew term for an all-encompassing
peace). This is exactly how baptism works: In baptism our truest
selves are revealed, an identity which can only be achieved fully in
the final consummation of the reign of God. It is from that place
of the truest self that God calls us. From our future, God beckons
us. Our responsibility is to make choices in line with that future.

What does this have to do with human dignity? Dignity as a
divine term is neither about the past nor the present. Dignity is not
earned, it is given. The realization of that dignity—both in myself,
in others, and indeed in the whole creation—is a lifelong pursuit.
Our full dignity, our full self as the image of God, is something we
are being drawn toward, as Johnson says, "from the future." This
process is called by some "sanctification." It's what Paul means
when he tells the Philippians to "work out your own salvation with

fear and trembling" (Phil. 2:12), and the Corinthians that they "are being transformed into the same image [of Christ] from one degree of glory to another" (2 Cor. 3:18). In the East this process is called *theosis* or "deification." Its most simple explanation was made by Athanasius (bishop of Alexandria who died in 373 CE): "[The Word of God] was made man that we might be made God."[21]

"That we might be made God" may sound like paganism, but it is an expression of statements made of or by Jesus in John's Gospel.

> To all who received him, who believed in his name, he gave power to become children of God, who were born not of blood, or of the will of the flesh, or of the will of man, but of God (John 1:12–13).

> The glory that you have given me I have given them, so that they may be one as we are one, I in them and you in me, that they may become completely one . . . I desire that those also, whom you have given me, may be with me where I am, to see my glory (John 17:22, 24).

Richard Hooker, as we saw earlier, would call this gift and destiny of humankind, "participation" in God.

Dignity is humanity's gift in the present and its destiny in the future. It is a result of God's grace and mercy, an expression of God's solidarity with the world and God's desire for human liberation. Hooker would say, however, that we not only participate in the life of God. We participate in one another's lives. Community is also our gift and destiny. Salvation, liberation, is a gift for all. We are made free together or we are not made free at all. South Africans call this *ubuntu*, the reality that I exist for you and you exist for me. I am because you are and *vice versa*. Archbishop Desmond Tutu explained *ubuntu* in his 1999 book, *No Future Without Forgiveness*.

> Ubuntu . . . speaks of the very essence of being human. [It means] you are generous, you are hospitable, you are friendly and caring and compassionate. You share what you have. It is to say "My humanity is caught up, is inextricably bound up, in yours." . . . We say, "A person is a person through other persons." It is not "I think therefore I am." It says rather: "I am human because I belong. I participate. I share." [I am] diminished when others are humiliated or diminished, when others are tortured or oppressed, or treated as if they were less than who they are.[22]

Here we discover why the Baptismal Covenant pairs striving for justice and peace with respecting the dignity of every human person. Dignity is the very presence of *shalom* in a person's life. This Hebrew term has a wider meaning than "peace," especially if you think of peace simply as the absence of conflict. *Shalom* is wholeness, well-being, freedom and, yes, dignity. Scripture asserts that human beings were created in the image of God. If *shalom* has an equivalent term in the New Testament, it is grace. Both *shalom* and grace are covenant words. They are found and nurtured in relationship with God and in community. Christian communities are intended to function as communities of *shalom* and grace, and to call and witness to this way of life together in the larger community.

William Temple saw this clearly and understood its ethical and political ramifications in the wider society.

The primary principle of Christian ethics and Christian politics must be respect for every person simply as a person. If each man and woman is a child of God, whom God loves and for whom Christ died, then there is in each a worth absolutely independent of usefulness to society. The person is primary, not the society; the State exists for the citizen, not the citizen for the State. . . . Freedom is the goal of politics. To establish and secure freedom is the primary object of all right political action. For it is in and through his freedom that a man makes fully real his personality—the quality of one made in the image of God. . . . Freedom so far as it is a treasure must be freedom *for* something as well as freedom *from* something. It must be the actual ability to form and carry out a purpose.[23]

Temple also saw where this commitment to human freedom and dignity goes wrong. Human freedom is open to abuse, because it is not so much a state of being as a way of life, a way in which choices must be made on a daily basis. These choices, moreover, are choices between my freedom and another's, and the human tendency to choose my freedom over others is as natural as breathing. It is impossible in this life to get it right all the time, perhaps even most of the time. But maturing in Christian faith, seeking to live in the fullness of life that our baptism exposes us to and promises us in the end, means seeking balance, of finding ways to live that uphold both my dignity and my neighbors, which bring as wide a scope of justice and peace as possible.

This process of seeking balance must be sought not only personally but publicly. The Christian's primary relation to the state is to call it to exercise its power to create an equitable society, one in which human freedom is nourished and human rights maintained, in a balance of beloved community. German theologian Jürgen Moltmann expects working toward these ends to be a struggle, but a struggle for which the Christian community is made. He uses an interesting phrase to describe the right of human dignity: the right of grace.

> By practicing the right of grace [Christians] practice basic human rights. The Christian faith does not excuse us from the struggle for the recognition and realization of human rights, but leads us into this very struggle. The community which calls Jesus "Son of Man" suffers under the ongoing inhumanity and dehumanization of human beings, and in its prayers turns this suffering into a painful awareness.[24]

Awareness of the other and the existence of suffering in the other is the essential first step in the practice of human dignity, brought about by justice and peace. It is not enough, but without honest awareness, we live increasingly self-centered lives, focusing only on our own pain, or denying that pain, and the pain of the other. Awareness fights amnesia and apathy, the great enemies of human dignity, and of the life of faith. Elizabeth Johnson asks, "If something consistently results in the denigration of human beings, in what sense can it be religiously true?"[25]

The Way of Wisdom

Wisdom cries out in the street; in the square she raises her voice. "How long, O simple ones, will you love being simple? How long will scoffers delight in their scoffing and fools hate knowledge?"

Proverbs 1:20–22

As is often the case in rural, farming communities, I was raised on the philosophy of pragmatism. Pragmatism is one part fatalism, one part tenacity, and one part hope. You deal with what the day, or the season, brings you. You keep the long view. You live with a great deal of paradox. You do everything you can to control how the crops grow, and how the animals produce, but you also know you are not in control, and are reminded of it frequently. If you are not consistently ready to learn, you will eventually fail. Farmers are among the wisest people I know, at least when they are not teetering on the edge of despair. Wisdom requires a certain amount of hope, believing that problems can be solved, and that knowledge ultimately prevails. It requires trust that putting seeds into the ground produces a crop, and this is the same trust that is required to live the long haul of life.

My great-great grandfather's first name was Duty, as was his grandfather's before him. My own grandfather's middle name was

Duty, as was his father's. I often wish it had been passed on to me. Yet even without the name, I inherited the value. I have chafed under it at times, especially when it has manifested itself as work-aholism, work "idolatry." But I learned over time that "duty" was not about how much work I did, but why I did it. The "why" of life, the motivation for our living, is much of what is meant by wisdom. Wisdom is the primary player in the next movement of Holy Baptism in the Book of Common Prayer.

We baptize in water, "In the Name of the Father, and of the Son, and of the Holy Spirit." That is the essential act of baptism, but it is not all that we have to say. After the water, there is an action with two parts: A prayer with the laying on of hands and the signing of the cross on the forehead of the newly baptized, usually done with an oil called "chrism," which has been blessed by the bishop.[1] The prayer gives thanks for what has just occurred, but then looks forward to the life that follows:

> Heavenly Father, we thank you that by water and the Holy Spirit you have bestowed upon these your servants the forgiveness of sins and have raised them to the new life of grace. Sustain them, O Lord, in your Holy Spirit. Give them an inquiring and sustaining heart, the courage to will and to persevere, a spirit to know and to love you, and the gift of joy and wonder in all your works.[2]

This prayer is often called the prayer for "the seven-fold gifts" of the Holy Spirit. These gifts are laid out in Isaiah 11:1–3.

A shoot shall come out from the stump of Jesse, and a branch shall grow out of his roots. The spirit of the LORD shall rest on him, the spirit of wisdom and understanding, the spirit of counsel and might, the spirit of knowledge and the fear of the LORD. His delight shall be in the fear of the LORD.

The seven-fold gifts in this passage have long been seen as the six pairs of verse 2: wisdom and understanding, counsel and might, and knowledge and fear of the Lord. The Septuagint, the Greek translation of the Scriptures available in Jesus's day, added "the spirit of piety" thus arriving at seven gifts. The prayer above uses the "delight" of verse 3 rather than "piety," and makes it a pairing in symmetry with the other three pairings—awe and wonder.

The prayer book prayer has a lovely simplicity to it, but it is unfortunate that the word "wisdom" has disappeared.[3] This is a crucial biblical term and one that in the Isaiah passage, seems to govern the rest of the attributes. The prayer as it appears in the previous prayer book of 1928 uses the word "wisdom," as do all major English translations of the Isaiah passage. There is no record that I can find of why the term was changed in the current prayer book. The biblical understanding of wisdom, however, is the true content of the prayer.

* * *

Wisdom in the Bible is often contrasted with "foolishness," as in the epigram to this chapter from Proverbs, which is the debut of Wisdom personified as a female figure through whom divine creativity and judgment are expressed. She appears throughout the first nine chapters of Proverbs, as well as in the apocryphal books of the Wisdom of Solomon, Sirach (Ecclesiasticus), and Baruch. Language and imagery about her are transferred to Jesus as the Word in John 1, and also is used in Colossians (1:15–20) and Hebrews (1:1–3).

Wisdom translated into both Hebrew (*ḥokmâh*) and Greek (*sophia*) is a feminine noun. Hence the biblical and apocryphal Wisdom is referred to as "she." Though not exactly equated with God, she is an expression of God's creativity and an interpreter of the ways of God. She is "a breath of the power of God, and a pure emanation of the glory of the Almighty" (Wisd. of Sol. 7:25). She is often equated with Torah (the Law in its broadest sense): "Hear the commandments of life, O Israel; give ear, and learn wisdom!" (Bar. 3:9). All the more reason for "wisdom" to appear in the prayer for the gifts of the Spirit, as an expression of the gender diversity within the divine. She is a witness to inclusion as a fundamental value of God.

The reasons behind the emergence of Wisdom as an expression of God's activity in the world has long been debated by scholars. It may well be that she was a response to the use of the feminine in the religions that surrounded ancient Israel. In this regard, she became increasingly important as the Jewish people began to spread throughout the Mediterranean region. The Wisdom tradition also gave language to God's immanence, God's vital presence and activity in the world, balancing the strong tradition of a transcendent God, a God above and beyond human experience. Wisdom says, "In the holy tent I ministered before [the Creator] and so I was established in Zion. Thus in the beloved city he gave me a resting place . . . I took root in an honored people" (Sir. 24:10–12). The early Christians adapted such language in order to speak about the incarnation of God in Jesus. The first chapter of John's Gospel speaks of "the Word" (*logos*) rather than Wisdom, but it is very clear the underlying concept and language is parallel. Note, for instance, the important phrase from John, "And the Word became flesh and lived among us." The Greek word translated "lived" refers to the pitching of a tent or tabernacle. It is the verbal form of the word "tent" in the quote from Sirach, above.

Knowing something about the language and figure of Wisdom in Jewish tradition is important in at least two ways. First, it emphasizes the continued action of God in the world, not only on behalf of humankind, but through it. Second, it disrupts patriarchal notions of God's call of humankind to act in the world. The call is equally to women and men, both made in the image of God. The call is to act with wisdom, but what does that mean in concrete terms?

Wisdom is more than simple "knowledge" or "understanding," although these are also listed as gifts of the Spirit, and wisdom certainly includes what we mean by those terms. Wisdom, akin to the Hebrew term for "peace" (*shalom*), is a much deeper and wider term. Like *shalom*, it bespeaks wholeness, not only of the self, but also of the community. Wisdom is the capacity to see beyond the self, to take into consideration both the learning of the ages and its practical implications over time. Walter Brueggemann refers to wisdom as "a body of accumulated teaching based on discernment and reflection about the character and mystery of life. . . . grounded in experience." "Wisdom literature," he says, "asks about 'what works,' what risks may be run, what realities can be trusted, and where the practice of human choice, human freedom, and human responsibility can be exercised."[4] Wisdom is pragmatic while never losing the long view, and holding the long view without losing the capacity for practical action.

* * *

The prayer for the seven-fold gifts of the Spirit is immediately followed by an anointing with oil. It is highly personal and specific: "You are sealed with the Holy Spirit in Baptism and marked as Christ's own for ever." They are among the most powerful words ever said over an individual in the Book of Common Prayer. They say the relationship that has been established in this rite is sealed. This relationship is a guarantee. You may doubt your relationship with God. You may get lost in spiritual apathy. You may even reject God. But God never goes away because the gift of God once given, remains forever. This truth is the source of any statement we might make concerning the dignity bestowed on the human creature by their Creator.

The gifts of the Spirit may be taken as a further explication of this giftedness, and they are certainly that. However, they also raise the question of responsibilities, of the duty bestowed with the dignity. "Wisdom" is an expression of both the giftedness and the responsibility. Evelyn Underhill, a twentieth-century Anglican writer, summarized the spiritual life as

An acceptance and living out of the actual, in its homeliest details and its utmost demands, in the light of the eternal; and with that peculiar sense of ultimate security which only a hold on the eternal can bring.[5]

Wisdom is lived. She is an expression of the life of the Spirit. She deals with the real and the true, not with fantasy or deception. She is a gift, and, therefore, to embrace her is to embrace an unshakeable confidence. The seal is forever, and this provides the "peculiar sense of security" of which Underhill speaks. Again, we are drawn to the prayer book's talk of baptism as the "indissoluble bond" with God.

We can rest in this bond, but it also must be lived. It comes with responsibilities, with a duty to God and neighbor which is also indissoluble. William Temple and the Christian Socialists of the late nineteenth and early twentieth centuries were adamant about the necessity of duty. Temple taught that there were three social principles endemic to Christianity, and, therefore to Christian ethics and politics: freedom, social fellowship, and service. Humankind is made for freedom, and it is in freedom that an individual "makes fully real his personality."[6] Human freedom is both freedom *from* anything that would depress human personality, and freedom *for* something, the carrying out of a purpose, ultimately a measure of the purposes of God.

Individuals are free to develop personality, but humankind is also inherently social, "naturally and incurably social," Temple says. Freedom's purpose is not solely self-interest; its highest expression is social. There is a balance between the individual and the community. Individuality is an expression of the rich diversity of creation and the varied gifts of God which make for uniqueness. Individuality (Temple uses the word "personality") is also social, and "only in his social relationships can man be a person. Indeed, for the completeness of personality, there is needed the relationship to both God and neighbours."[7] We are back to the notion of *ubuntu*, an aspect of which is, "I am because I serve."

The balance between individual and community, freedom and fellowship, Temple says, "issues in the obligation of service."[8] The primary question for the Christian Socialists was not, "What does my neighbor owe me?" but "What do I owe my neighbor?" Individuality is not only the way in which one expresses one's difference from others, but how one's make-up is given by God so that each person may uniquely serve others.

The balance between individuality and the obligation to community is often described in the language of human rights. Use of this language, however, varies widely. For many, human rights are understood primarily as individuals' right to determine the course of their own lives, ultimately to do with their lives whatever seems right to them. In other contexts, human rights consist of the right to the basics of human life—clean water, education, health care, housing, etc.

The latter understanding is very much the basis for the Universal Declaration of Human Rights, one of the first major acts of the United Nations at its inception.[9] The rights delineated over the thirty articles of the declaration are largely those of everyday living. In the words of the declaration's preamble, they serve to protect "the inherent dignity and . . . the equal and inalienable right of all members of the human family." They are "the foundation of freedom, justice and peace in the world." There is a balance, however, as expressed in Article 29: "Everyone has duties to the community in which alone the free and full development of his [sic] personality is possible."

Biblically and theologically, human rights derive from the unique creation and call of each individual. "You are sealed by the Holy Spirit . . . and marked as Christ's own for ever." Yet human rights must always be balanced by human responsibilities. "I am who I am" must go hand in hand with "I am who I serve." My individuality is called to the service of others. There is no more basic Christian principle.

The responsibility toward others must be exercised with respect and dignity. Service of others cannot be called Christian if it does not result in heightened respect and dignity for the other. Service itself can become an idol if it is done for self-aggrandizement. Rowan Williams, looking to St. Antony of the Desert and seeing the connection between respect for others and a right relationship with the divine, observes:

> St. Antony . . . says that gaining the brother or sister and winning God are linked. It is not getting them signed up to something or getting them on your side. It is opening doors for them to healing and to wholeness. Insofar as you open doors for another, you gain God, in the sense that you become a place where God happens for somebody else. *You become a place where God happens.* . . . not because you are good and wonderful but because that is what God has done.[10]

You become a place where God happens. This is the new life of grace. This is being immersed in the Wisdom of God, to have a discerning heart, the courage to persevere, and to embrace the gift of joy and wonder. It is the answer to St. Paul's urgent question, "Do you not know that you are God's temple and that God's Spirit dwells in you?" (1 Cor. 3:16).

When we claim that we "are sealed by the Holy Spirit and marked as Christ's own for ever," we mean both that God will never let go of us, and that God will never stop calling us. More than that: We mean that God will never stop working through us, working through us *for a purpose*. This is not "the purpose driven life," a phrase popular in some evangelical circles. It is not a purpose that is primarily for my own benefit, as in some sort of "prosperity gospel." God working through us for a purpose is *always for the common good*.

We should understand ourselves as part of that common good, of course. God wants us as individuals to thrive. Jesus said, "I came that they may have life, and have it abundantly" (John 10:10). Irenaeus of Lyon, writing in the late second century, declared *Gloria Dei vivens homo*, "the glory of God is the living human."[11] Yet there can be no doubt that the Bible and the writings of the early Church fathers universally see the common good as the divine priority. We need look no farther than the *Letter to Diognetus*, from which we quoted in chapter 2: "To be happy does not consist in lording it over one's neighbors . . . If a man takes his neighbor's burden on himself . . . then this man is an imitator of God."[12] Or, from a couple centuries later, St. Ambrose: "Not from your own do you bestow upon the poor, but you make return from what is his. For what has been given as common for the use of all, you appropriate to yourself alone. The earth belongs to all, not to the rich . . . Therefore you are paying a debt, you are bestowing what is due."[13]

The common good has no limiting definition. It does not refer to tribe or party or nation. Even though Israel frequently thought of itself in exclusive terms when it came to relationship with the God who was revealed to Abraham and Moses, the prophets push against this exclusiveness. Isaiah says Israel is to be a light for the nations (Isa. 42:6). When Jesus is presented in the Temple, Simeon sings that the child will be "a light for revelation to the Gentiles" (Luke 2:32). The revelation of the Messiah to the Gentiles (i.e., the whole world) becomes the primary mission of St. Paul. The Bible ends with visions from the Book of Revelations, including this song:

> And yours by right, O Lamb that was slain,
>> for with your blood you have redeemed for God,
> from every family, language, people, and nation,
>> a royal priesthood to serve our God.[14]

Our English phrase "common good" has everything to do with the Bible's vision of *shalom*, of which I have spoken already. Here I want to make the connection between wisdom, *shalom*, and the common good. When Wisdom cries out in the street at the beginning of Proverbs, it is this vision which is the background of her cry, and fools are those who refuse to embrace this vision and reject the ways of Wisdom as folly. She decries the "simple," the "scoffers," and "fools who hate knowledge."

In our common life—including in our politics—Wisdom cries out for us to embrace the truth, not as we would have it, but as it really is. To create one's own truth is often to take pieces of truth and stitch them together with deceptions and lies. We "scoff" at truth because it does not fit into our worldview, which is almost always too simple in its understanding of the world, ourselves, and God. J. B. Phillips's classic Christian guide is titled *Your God Is Too Small.*[15] We might reasonably add, "Your truth is too small."

If truth is one side of a coin, then mystery is on the other side of it. The bane of much of our public life is that mystery is a vast part of the truth, the world as God would have it. Every public servant—and every one of us in our social thinking—needs to have God's questions of Job in the forefront of our mind: "Who is this that darkens counsel by words without knowledge? Where were you when I laid the foundation of the earth?" (Job 38:1 & 4).

Only in a mutually respectful acknowledgement of the mystery of life can disagreements be worked through, and compromises reached for the common good. Our political life shipwrecks every time we approach one another as if each side had divinely inspired opinions on right and wrong. This is not to say that as individuals and groups we should avoid points of view, some about which we are passionate. To do so is only human. But God calls us to more. And this "more" is primarily to do with the process of our conversations with one another. We recognize one another's convictions, courage, and knowledge. We take the time to learn of one another's wonder and joy, because it is often when we do so we begin to see paths forward together.

The seven-fold gifts of the Spirit have an equivalent New Testament passage in St. Paul's Letter to the Galatians:

> The fruit of the Spirit is love, joy, peace, patience, kindness, generosity, faithfulness, gentleness, and self-control. There is no law against such things. . . . If we live by the Spirit, let us also be guided by the Spirit. Let us not become conceited, competing against one another, envying one another. (Gal. 5:22–23, 25–26)

Imagine our public life—local, national, global—if these words guided our interactions. Many will say that conceit, competition, and envy are especially endemic to politics and there is no way to implement the fruit of the Spirit into our political life. Yet to say so and to act so is to give up on the very basics of both Jewish and Christian faith.

Lady Wisdom is the principal figure of the Book of Proverbs in its first nine chapters. She begins, as we began this chapter, in the streets with the pronouncement against folly. She ends with a banquet, to which she invites the simple and "those without sense:"

> Wisdom has built her house, she has hewn her seven pillars. She has slaughtered her animals, she has mixed her wine, she has also set her table. She has sent out her servant-girls, she calls from the highest places in the town, "You that are simple, turn in here!" To those without sense she says, "Come, eat of my bread and drink of the wine I have mixed. Lay aside immaturity, and live, and walk in the way of insight." (Prov. 9:1–6)

The way of insight could also be termed the way of holiness. Rowan Williams writes of the habits of holiness in his book about St. Benedict's Rule. Holiness is not primarily about piety. "The holy person," Williams says, "struggles to live without deceit . . . who makes peace by addressing the roots of conflict in him or herself, [and] attempts to contribute their distinctive gifts in such a way as to sustain healthy 'circulation' in the community."[16] He points out that St. Benedict's Rule exhorts the person under vows "not be enthralled to satisfying fictions about yourself . . . to accept responsibility in the way things are and the way things go wrong.[17]

This can be done only in community, in what St. Paul calls "the Body of Christ" (from which Williams gets his notion of "healthy circulation"), and which the baptismal rite in the Book of Common Prayer calls "the household of God."

CHAPTER 9

The Way of Belonging

To pray is to build your own house. To pray is to discover that Someone else is within your house. To pray is to recognize it is not your house at all. To keep praying is to have no house to protect because there is only One House. And that One House is everybody's Home. That is the politics of prayer. And it is probably why truly spiritual people are always a threat to politicians of any sort. They want our allegiance and we can no longer give it. Our house is too big.

—Richard Rohr, "Prayer as Political Activity"

In the summer of 1990, I was called to be the vicar of St. George's Chapel in Glenn Dale, Maryland. St. George's had begun its life in 1873 as a "chapel of ease" of a nearby parish. Chapels of ease were common in those days in the mid-Atlantic. They remained under the umbrella of the sponsoring parish, served by the same clergy. In the late 1950s the parish gave St. George's to the Diocese of Washington and it became a diocesan mission. Its character remained largely unchanged, however. When I was called there were forty or so members of the congregation. The 100-year-old carpenter gothic building didn't seat many more than that.

In the time between when I was called and when I was scheduled to begin ministry with them, I was outed as a gay man.

The leadership—along with the patriarch and matriarch of the congregation—decided to go ahead with their call, even though three people quite loudly protested and left the congregation. We did not have a great deal of conversation about what my being gay would mean for the parish. Their only concern was that I not be a "flag waver." I was told the only real concern expressed among some of the members was that I might bring a large number of gay people to the congregation and change its character. I assured them that would not happen. If nothing else, Glenn Dale was an outer suburb of Washington, DC. The likelihood of people driving out of the city to come to church there was miniscule. And everyone assumed, of course, that no gay people lived in the suburbs, or at least none who wished to be known as such.

I was there for about three years when the first gay person showed up, a lesbian who lived not far from the church. At some point after her arrival, I took her aside and told her how glad I was to have a "member of the family" join the congregation. Unfortunately, that remark was overheard and spread. Soon I had angry people who heard in my remark that I did not consider them family and that my goal was to create a new family at St. George's, replacing them. It was a definite error on my part, although it also revealed a tendency toward defensiveness in the church, a defensiveness that almost always results in a vision of the church that is too small.

We got through the crisis because we talked openly about it, let people express their fears, checked our perceptions with the biblical record, and made the choice to trust one another. I spent a total of fourteen years at St. George's, enough time for us to grow, build a new, larger, church, and become a full-fledged parish, all built on the inclusiveness of the gospel. This inclusiveness is enacted in the baptismal rite as the congregation welcomes the newly baptized.

* * *

After the anointing in the baptismal rite, the congregation acts to include the newly baptized in the assembly. They say,

> We receive you into the household of God. Confess the faith of Christ crucified, proclaim his resurrection, and share with us in his eternal priesthood.

The metaphor for the church this act of reception uses is not family, but "the household of God." The biblical source for this metaphor is primarily Ephesians 2:19: "So then you are no longer strangers and aliens, but you are citizens with the saints and also members of the household of God." Galatians 6:10, 1 Timothy 3:15, and 1 Peter 4:17 also use this metaphor.

The Greek word used in these places is a form of *oikos*, which can mean the triad of house, household, and the management of the household. While it can be translated "family," most English translations (beginning with the King James version) do not do so. The reasons are twofold, I think. One, there is a strong desire to keep the three uses of the word connected in English as they are in Greek. Two, our use of the word family tends to be quite different from the experience of household in the ancient world. We hear the word family and think primarily of the nuclear family of spouses, usually with children, and, secondarily, of those related by blood and/or marriage. An ancient household encompassed both these meanings and more, including slaves, servants, apprentices, and others. The New Testament goes even further, especially in Ephesians 2, which speaks of breaking down dividing walls and ending hostilities between peoples. In Christ, whom Ephesians says "is our peace" (2:14), Jews and Gentiles are members of the same household. There is only one household in this vision, the household gathered (to use Jesus's words) "from east and west, from north and south, [who] will eat in the kingdom of God" (Luke 13:29, cf. Matt. 8:11).

Oikos is a vitally important word for us to understand in our contemporary setting. The English words "economy" and "economics" (also, in a different context, "ecumenical") are derived from *oikos*. These words pick up on the aspect of *oikos* that engages the managers of the household, sometimes translated as "stewards."[1] This tie between household and economy in New Testament language is instructive. Contemporary economics, especially in its practice (as opposed to theory), too often ignores the vital link between the household economy and the large-scale economy of corporate practice and the modern obsession with the stock market. When the state of the stock market is more important than the state of the household, we have turned our back on the biblical vision.

The Bible's vision is the notion of stewardship rather than ownership. From one of the first words we learn as toddlers—"mine"—to our national/international addiction with acquiring things to call our own, we show that we do not accept the biblical understanding that "all things come from thee, O Lord, and of thine own have we given thee."[2] Any gift we give—to anyone or to any person—is a gift we have received and passed on. God as Creator is God the Giver, exclusively so.

The implications of this view of God as Giver and we human beings as stewards, "householders," of God's gifts, are many and serious. The image summoned is corporate. God gives gifts to individuals, of course, but only to individuals-in-community: "We receive you into the household of God . . . share with us . . ." To live in this vision of a household and world where all is shared requires constant decision-making that more frequently than not goes against societal norms, which tend to assume a very high level of individual autonomy. In that autonomy, values of freedom are held dear, but we are also led to view others as competitors in a world ruled by scarcity.

In his commentary on *The Rule of St. Benedict*, Rowan Williams speaks of Benedict's vision of community applied to the contemporary church:

> We are sisters and brothers in the Church not because we naturally and instinctively belong together, agree, or speak the same language, but because we are summoned to be together in our strangeness to each other. And to be faithful to each other in that strangeness—not because we naturally like one another and would be loyal to one another anyway![3]

In such a community, Williams says, two things must be true. Our commitment to the common good must be unambiguous, although this does not mean accepting a predetermined uniformity of thought and action. It means, rather, that every perspective is important, *and* every perspective is open to challenge. This can only succeed when there is an equal commitment to refuse "any sort of competitive struggle for the dominance of one individual or group."[4]

This competitive struggle is an apt description of our public life; it seems to be its very point most of the time, with only rare moments of open communication, questioning, and arriving at something that benefits the common good. This often manifests in party politics. It seems natural—what does having political parties mean if it is not to compete, to prove your side right and the other wrong? Yet this very notion of a fundamentally competitive world of winners and losers is what we are called to overcome. We are called instead into the strange world of the common good, a community of strangers who nevertheless choose to live together and to trust each other even when they disagree.

In more explicitly spiritual terms, our competitiveness is fueled by the human need to justify oneself or one's group, to assert the rightness of one's cause, of the decisions made day by day that exert one's freedom, freedom that is both hard won and hard kept. But this embattled vision is not by any means aligned with the biblical and sacramental understanding of freedom. Sacramental freedom is a gift for us to receive, not a status we are required to earn. "The church," Williams says, "is a community that exists because something has happened that makes the entire process of self-justification irrelevant."[5]

This "something" that has happened is the life, death, and resurrection of Jesus Christ. Baptism puts us into this very different process: In the water of baptism, "we are buried with Christ in his death . . . [and] share in his resurrection . . . [and] are reborn by the Holy Spirit."[6] This new life (St. Paul calls it "a new creation") is a life lived not only for self, but for others, patterned on

Jesus's own life. Like Jesus's own way of living, the patterning of our life after his will not be received well by everyone. It will often be risky, and lead, if not to death itself, at least to little deaths, times of letting go of the values of this world which may lead to misunderstanding or even scorn on the part of those who do not accept it.

* * *

The reception of the newly baptized gives us another image to help us understand what living this way of common, shared life entails. We invite the newly baptized to "share with us in [Christ's] eternal priesthood."

"Priest" is a slippery image, especially in the churches who use the term to designate individuals who are ordained to lead communities of faith in the ministry of word and sacrament. There is, however, a more foundational use of the term, often referred to as "the priesthood of all believers." This is the priesthood that both the New Testament and the sacramental life begun in baptism calls us to share. It is a priesthood that flows from Jesus Christ, himself "our great high priest." The Letter to the Hebrews includes a long section (chapters 2–10) laying out what it means that Jesus is the ultimate—and final—high priest.[7] This section begins with a thesis statement (Heb. 2:17):

> [Jesus] had to become like his brothers and sisters in every respect, so that he might be a merciful and faithful high priest in the service of God, to make a sacrifice of atonement for the sins of the people.

In the larger world of religious language, the term "priest" is often connected with the word "sacrifice." Making sacrifices to God or the gods is what priests did to appease the divine. This usually involved the spilling of blood, nay, the taking of a life. One of the main points of the Letter to the Hebrews is that Jesus is the last and eternal priest in this regard. His blood spilt is the last blood that ever need be spilt in the name of religion. But what does it mean for the baptized to share in this eternal priesthood?

Looking at the statement of Hebrews 2:17, we can identify several things. First, to be a priest is to share life with others. The priesthood of Christ is fundamentally social. As William Countryman says, "True priestly service cannot be offered out of condescension, but only out of a shared identity."[8] This shared identity is characterized in Hebrews 2:17 in two ways, as "merciful" and as "faithful." Second, priests are in the service of God, not—by implication—themselves. Third, the goal of priestly sacrifice or offering is "atonement," that is, reconciliation between God and humankind. The logic of the statement is circular. The reconciliation is not only between God and humankind, but among humans, in solidarity with one another. This is the very definition of the church's mission in the Book of Common Prayer: "to restore all persons to unity with God and each other in Christ" (The Book of Common Prayer, p. 855).

The priesthood of all the baptized is a priesthood that is shared, not a collection of priests. This is the vision of the First Letter of Peter:

> Come to him, a living stone . . . and like living stones, let yourselves be built into a spiritual house, to be a holy priesthood, to offer spiritual sacrifices acceptable to God through

Jesus Christ. . . . You are a chosen race, a royal priesthood, a holy nation, God's own people, in order that you may proclaim the mighty acts of him who called you out of darkness into his marvelous light. (1 Pet. 2:4–5, 9–10)[9]

This passage very neatly puts together the two images from the reception in Holy Baptism: "house" and "priest." The Church is a "household of priests." We are called to exercise our priesthood in the same way as Jesus, the high priest, in solidarity with all humanity and in the service of God (a higher purpose than we ourselves can muster), to be witnesses to the unity God desires with humanity and that God desires for all humankind to share. I say "witnesses," because we do need to take care that we do not imagine ourselves to create this unity. Unity, reconciliation, and atonement are gifts from God. If anything, we are called to uncover and live in what already is by the high priesthood of Jesus Christ.

As priests we are called to offer the world to God through Jesus Christ in the power of the Holy Spirit. A hymn text makes this clear:

Lord, you make the common holy:
"This my body, this my blood."
Let your priests, for earth's true glory,
daily lift life heavenward,
asking that the world around us,
share your children's liberty;
with the Spirit's gifts empower us
for the work of ministry.[10]

The author may have intended "priests" here to refer to the ordained priesthood, but it equally applies to the priesthood of all. Note that the task of "lifting life heavenward" is for the benefit of the world in the present moment. The purpose, furthermore, is stated in a way that may surprise us, so that the world might "share your children's liberty." Yes, this refers to freedom in Christ, but it is impossible to use words like "liberty" and "freedom" without an earthly content, and, it must be said, a social one, with both political and economic consequences.

Evelyn Underhill cites an image from Dante which is relevant here, noting that as soon as "a soul ceases to say Mine, and says Ours, it makes the transition from the narrow, constricted, individual life to the truly free, truly personal, truly creative spiritual life."[11] She is adamant that the spiritual life is not separate from day-to-day practical living. The spiritual life is not something "specialized and intense." We are not separated from the world, but rather immersed in it. We are called to an intensely social life that emulates the life of the Trinity. She writes that in the living of Dante's "Ours," "All interpenetrate, and all, however humble or obscure their lives may seem, can and do affect each other. Every advance made by one is made for all."[12]

The priesthood of all believers is inherently social. To live into this priesthood requires close attention to relationships and a keen understanding of, and watchfulness for, the giftedness of all. Out of these relationships flow the energy, the compassion, and the grace needed to act for the common good in the world.

* * *

We have now examined the images at the beginning and end of the welcome of the newly baptized. In the middle lies the imperative of proclamation: "Confess the faith of Christ crucified, proclaim his resurrection . . ."This imperative is linked to the earlier commitment of the Baptismal Covenant to "proclaim by word and example the Good News of God in Christ." Schillebeeckx sees in Jesus's death a radical solidarity with humankind and, indeed, the whole world. The cross proclaims, "A God of human beings, an ally in our suffering and our absurdity, an ally too in the good that we do."[13] This is the image from John's Gospel; of Jesus with his arms stretched out on the cross to draw the whole world to himself. It is an understanding of the cross as the culmination of Jesus's life. The life and death of Jesus must be seen as "a single entity."[14] To speak of the cross as a sacrifice, only makes sense when it is the outcome of a sacrificial life.

Schillebeeckx goes on to speak of the resurrection as announcing and enacting four realities, each building on the other:[15]

- Resurrection faith is "an evangelical evaluation of Jesus's life and crucifixion." Jesus's proclamation and practice of what he called the kingdom of God is affirmed.

- The resurrection is the definitive instance of what had been clear in Jesus's life from the beginning: Communion with God is not only possible, it is unbreakable.

- The resurrection establishes Jesus as the glorified Lord of Life for those who would follow him, and exclusively so.

- Resurrection faith asserts that "the crucified but risen Jesus remains at work in our history." "Jesus is alive" is not the proclamation of a moment in history. It is the proclamation of an ever-present, eternal reality. The Church's faith is that Christ *is* risen, not Christ *has* risen.

The life, passion, death, and resurrection of Jesus is often referred to as "The Paschal Mystery." Life–death–new life is the pattern Christians see not only in Jesus's life but in all life. It is the pattern of God's longing for creation, and humankind as part of it, to live as one, because only as one can we fully experience new life. This new life means living as the household of God, sharing in Christ's life, death, and resurrection, and living as priests who offer their whole lives and the life of the world to the Giver of Life.

The household of God is not only the place where God's longing can find its creative expression. It is a place where human longing can do so as well. And this depends on a broad understanding of and commitment to belonging. Furthermore, human belonging as the vision and practice of Christians is a social and political vision, one which witnesses to the world of relationships as God would have them.

Peter Selby, sometime bishop of Worcester in the Church of England, wrote of this witness in a book called, simply, *BeLonging*. "The Church," he wrote, "is placed in the world to express the longing of God. If that is so, it has to have a different way of being community from that which we see in other human communities." In the world, there is a tendency, he observes, "to achieve a sense of belonging generally at someone else's expense." In each of the synoptic Gospels (and twice in Luke!) a dispute arose among the disciples about who was the greatest.[16] The tale is told in slightly different ways, but in each one Jesus says, "But not among you." The way of competitiveness, the desire to be "greater than," and the way of exclusion to achieve this end is the way of the world. One belongs by being "different than." In contrast, Selby says, the witness of Christians must be that "What are excluded are only those things which themselves result in holding back God's concern to include." Of course, he admits, the church throughout history has succumbed to the temptation of exclusion in order to define itself.[17]

As part of that conversation in my first parish, the question was raised as to how far "inclusion" is to go. Are there no limits? After a lot of back and forth, one of our oldest members put the question to rest: "Everyone's welcome at the table, except those who would tear it down."

When the church practices exclusion, it is violating its baptismal creed, and, indeed, its whole reason for being. We have too often been a witness to the "proper" way to determine who is worthy and who is not, usually based either on heresy (holding wrong belief) or sinfulness (practicing wrong morality). That this is still the way of much of the church is a tragedy, a shameful witness to the world and at least part of the reason for the rise of the "nones," those who reject the institutional church in all its forms.

The way of the world is too often alienation, not reconciliation—belonging—and with frequently deadly consequences. Episcopal priest and theologian Kelly Brown Douglas calls out this commitment to alienation as what she names a "stand-your-ground culture."

Stand-your-ground culture alienates people from the very goodness of their own creation. It essentially turns people in on themselves as it sets people against one another. This culture promotes the notion that one life has more value than another life. This is a culture that thrives on antagonistic relationships as signaled by the very idea of "standing one's ground." A stand-your-ground culture does not value dialogue, mutuality, respect, or compassion.[18]

Being true to our baptismal creed and covenant is the only antidote we have to the competitive and exclusive cultural impulse that is so alive in our world and in some parts of the church. The belief in God and in our shared responsibility to act on God's behalf as expressed in the Baptismal Covenant must be held in all humility and a witness not only to our actions within the church, but without it as well. The practice of belonging is the right practice of baptism, and of its repeated celebration of the Eucharist.

CHAPTER 10

The Way of Communion

[This] is . . . one function of the eucharistic table: to practice regularly the intentional violation of the customary boundaries that separate us.

—Sam Portaro, *Crossing the Jordan*

Nearly all Episcopalians, as well as those in other sacramental traditions, experienced a shift in reality beginning in March 2020, when we were prevented from celebrating the Eucharist due to the COVID-19 pandemic. I came to think of it as the eucharistic desert. By the time of this writing, close to three years later, almost all of us have returned to public celebrations, although many still receive the consecrated bread only. Some, especially the elderly and others with medical conditions that make them particularly vulnerable to the virus, have not been physically present in church for three years, and we look to be coming up on our fourth Easter without fully being able to gather as a body.[1]

For a while I, like everyone else, gave it a "stiff upper lip" and participated in online platform services. I prayed the prayers for spiritual communion along with everyone else. It wasn't long, however, that I became nothing short of miserable. I felt as if my spirituality was being shaken to its core. I became an Episcopalian as the 1979 version of the Book of Common Prayer was coming into use. My spirituality developed as I was taught the new prayer book intended that the Eucharist is "the principal act of Christian worship on the Lord's Day."[2] A colleague suggested I was missing the point of this time away from the Eucharist, which was to remind the church that Jesus is available to us spiritually at any time and in any place. Theoretically, I get what he meant. The suggestion, however, did not help me—I was spiritually starving. It was not the reception of communion alone I was missing. I was missing the dynamics of doing so *together*. I was feeling separated from the body and its fundamental practice around the eucharistic table. In forty years of celebrating the Eucharist, it had never stopped forming my spirit, through the dynamics caused by our mutual participation in living "the Lord's death until he comes."

I do not mean to suggest that online participation in the Eucharist is somehow less than physical participation. And isn't online participation still physical? There are, after all, bodies on the other side of those view screens. Nearly everyone wants participation through these alternate means to remain an option, but we are still trying to wrap our minds around just what "spiritual communion" is. One writer in a recent *Worship* journal has suggested that we are really talking about "the desire for communion."[3] The distinction may be important, especially if one is talking about communion in the larger sense of the Body of Christ, the household of God.

Holy Baptism is a singular event. It is not repeated, unlike the Eucharist. The Holy Eucharist is the fundamental way we practice the mystery of the new people, as laid out by baptism, and are fed to live it out in the world. Perhaps it is the case that our weekly celebration of the Eucharist hinders our remembrance of this truth, although I have my doubts about this hypothesis. I rather chalk it up to fuzzy teaching and preaching. We ought frequently to be reminded that, as Episcopal priest Sam Portaro says, the Eucharist is our "regular intentional violation of the customary boundaries that separate us," or, as writer Annie Dillard has observed,

> On the whole, I do not find Christians, outside of the catacombs, sufficiently sensible of conditions. Does anyone have the foggiest idea what sort of power we so blithely invoke? Or, as I suspect, does no one believe a word of it? The churches are children playing on the floor with their chemistry sets, mixing up a batch of TNT to kill a Sunday morning. It is madness to wear ladies' straw hats and velvet hats to church; we should all be wearing crash helmets. Ushers should issue life preservers and signal flares; they should lash us to our pews. For the sleeping god may wake someday and take offense, or the waking god may draw us out to where we can never return.[4]

Or, as I suggested in a sermon not long ago, we really should post a warning on our doors that "an upside-down world awaits you within." That many of us rarely have that experience in church is a problem. Some of the first pastoral advice I received after being ordained was, "Don't scare the horses very often." I think now it is not so much about not scaring them as it is keeping them awake, keeping them alive to the expectation that God is doing something here that makes a difference in real lives lived in the real world.

The Eucharist is at once both mundane and mystical. It invites us deep within ourselves, but it does so using the most worldly of things: bread and wine, food and drink. It sends us out into the world, but it does so with us bearing the life of God *and* with eyes to see the life of God at work in the mundane. We bring that to everyday work, with its moments of glory and its moments of falling short, back to the eucharistic assembly around the table for renewal. The Eucharist is a process. Followers of Jesus became convinced very early on that the command, "Do this in remembrance of me," implied a repetition. This remembrance was to be done again and again. So, St. Paul, writing only twenty to twenty-five years after the crucifixion, adds a crucial adverb to Jesus's command, 'osakis, "as often," or, as is the translation in most contemporary eucharistic prayers, "whenever."

The eucharistic process favors neither an individualistic spirituality nor a communal one. It is a balance of both, but it is more accurate to say that it knows of this distinction not at all. The Eucharist can never be the act of an individual.[5] It is fundamentally a social act, although the "society" is always a collection of individuals. And, as we have emphasized over and over again, if the act is social, it is also by definition political.

The social and political nature of this act has, at times, had negative consequences. As Lauren Winner points out in her book, *The Dangers of Christian Practice*, the Eucharist became tied to violent acts against Jews.[6] This developed over time—reaching its height in the Middle Ages, though not unheard of today—as devotion to the elements of the Eucharist came to be as important, or more, than their reception. By the late thirteenth century, Winner observes, accusations that Jews had stolen and desecrated a consecrated host were commonplace, and often led to violence.[7]

From earliest days baptism and Eucharist were rites of identification. They were characteristic acts of the followers of Jesus Christ, as they still are. It is another step to understand these two sacramental acts to be creators of social and political boundaries, as if what the Eucharist projected onto the life of the world were the definitive boundaries that determine social inclusion and even the right to live and die. That is a far cry from the experience of the Eucharist as the uncovering of the divine in all of life. It makes sense that the Eucharist is the characteristic act of a particular community. However, it does not make sense that it sets the moral and political boundaries of society, outside the followers of Jesus's participation in that society.

The Eucharist (and Christian worship in general) is intended to create a people who are active in the world, agents for change that are inspired by their faith in the Crucified and Risen One. Attention must be made to the *nature* of that change. There are many ways to express it. The Baptismal Covenant in the Book of Common Prayer is, at least for Episcopalians, the definitive description. The change we seek in the world is first grounded in a story (summarized by the Apostles' Creed), in the ongoing practice of worship (especially "the breaking of the bread"), and prayer and honest reflection, both on the individual and the communal level. This story and discipline commit us to a message that is good news. We seek the divine life in our neighbors (defined without exclusion) and engage a lifestyle that upholds the dignity of all life by the exercise of justice and peace.

There is no sense of division there, and to those who question whether this is a truly biblical understanding of the Christian life, one need only read St. Paul's list of the gifts of the Spirit in

Galatians: love, joy, peace, patience, kindness, generosity, faithfulness, gentleness, and self-control. Division, that is, "enmities, strife, jealousy, anger, quarrels, dissensions, factions, and envy" are, for Paul, "works of the flesh" (Gal. 5:19–21).

That our current public life is clearly dominated by these "works of the flesh" is obvious, and perhaps an understatement. That the vast majority of those practicing the politics of social division are at least nominally Christian is, or ought to be, a great scandal. And it looks like it is. In terms of religious practice, the twenty-first century is proving to be a time of rapid growth for those claiming no affiliation with institutional religion (the "spiritual but not religious") and those claiming to have no religious or spiritual tradition at all, those "nones" of which we have already spoken.

According to Pew Research, in 2021, 63 percent of Americans called themselves Christians, down fifteen percentage points since 2007. "Other religions" constitute 6 percent (up one percentage point since 2007). "No religion" is now the answer to the pollsters of 29 percent of the U.S. population, up thirteen points. By far the greatest hit is being taken by Protestants, down 12 percent, but even Roman Catholics are down 3 percent. Arguably a more important figure applies to those who consider religion "important" in their lives. It is at 41 percent, down from 56 percent in 2007.[8]

Why the precipitous decline? It's beyond the scope of this book to go into a deep analysis. Anecdotally, many claim that Christianity's entanglement with politics is currently fueling these declines. Most of the public doesn't understand the difference between evangelical and liberal Christians[9] in this regard, making liberals guilty by association. Yet even among liberal Christians, some would like the church to divorce itself from politics altogether. The very purpose of this book is to offer a different perspective from this reaction.

To understand the decline, we must first acknowledge the history of abuse that the church carries. For more than twenty years there has been a seemingly endless string of cases of sexual assault on behalf of church leaders, or those leaders covering it up. The abuse suffered by indigenous people at the hands of Christian missionaries is staggering. We are still dealing with the legacy of many Christians' support of slavery. Anti-Semitism continues in the wake of the Holocaust, a horrific enactment of centuries of violent prejudice. These abuses, and other misuses of power, are betrayals of the good news of God in Jesus Christ, and the church can only reply with humility, repentance, and restoration. This history—and its ongoing manifestations—seriously compromises the church's message, as well it should. We will recover, but only after much painful honesty and a very public commitment to reconciliation.

Yet there has been another truth, one of faithful living, and we must not lose sight of what we argued above: Baptism makes a people (a *polis*) and Eucharist re-makes them over and over again, for the purpose of living a particular way of life in the world. As Anglican priest and liturgical scholar Dom Gregory Dix wrote amid the liturgical renewal movement of the early to mid-twentieth century, "One could fill many pages with the reasons why men have done this, and not tell a hundredth part of them. And best of all, week by week and month by month, on a hundred thousand successive Sundays, faithfully, unfailingly, across all the parishes of Christendom, the pastors have done this just to *make* the *plebs sancta Dei*—the holy common people of God."[10]

It is the "holy common people of God" who can save the church by their service in acting for justice and peace, displaying an unshakeable and unequivocal commitment to the dignity of not only all human beings, but all creatures, and the earth itself. The church as an institution cannot do this. There is not enough trust of institutions in our time, a fact we often bemoan, but we must understand and accept that we have earned this lack of trust. The role of the institution and its leaders must be to quietly and clearly encourage, equip, and support the actions of the common people of God for the common good.

We keep wanting to be saved by charismatic, even messianic, leaders. This may provide some institutional revival here and there. But what we need is the formation of a charismatic and messianic people—a people who use their God-given gifts (i.e., "charismatic") for the liberation of humankind and the world (i.e., "messianic"). The institution's main role in the foreseeable future is to form followers of Jesus committed to Jesus's lifestyle and vision of the common good.

It is time to go back to the questions raised at the beginning of this book.

CHAPTER 11

The Way of Peace

> *What we can say [to the world] is that here are the signs by*
> *which we measure social, communal health—and its absence.*
> *That's the heart of what the Christian community . . . says in*
> *the political sphere.*
>
> —Rowan Williams, *The Rule of St. Benedict*

At the end of the first chapter, I asked three questions: What is the responsibility of a Christian in public life? What do words like politics and economics mean for a Christian? What does participation in the public life of the nation, or of the world, have to do with what Bishop Michael Curry calls, "participating in the Jesus Movement?" It's time to attempt an answer, given all the sources to which we have been led by the rite of Holy Baptism in the Book of Common Prayer.

But first, a story. Paul Jones was the bishop of Utah from 1914 to 1918. Today he is commemorated on the calendar of The Episcopal Church with a "lesser feast" on September 4, the day of his death in 1941. The feast is a kind of apology, a recognition that Paul Jones was treated badly by his peers, more or less silenced for what he had to say, thoughts that a later generation determined to be important.

Jones was both a socialist and a pacifist. The former was not so unusual. We have heard from many in both The Episcopal Church and the Church of England who had a socialist bent in the latter half of the nineteenth century and first half of the twentieth century. However, pacifism was not as acceptable either in society or in the church, especially once "the Great War" began.

Jones volunteered to serve in the missionary diocese of Utah upon his ordination in 1906. Within the diocese was Fort Douglas, which served as a detention center for pacifists and, as the United States entered World War I, one of two detention centers in the United States for German nationals who had been classified as "enemy aliens." This internment is not as well-known as the Japanese internment during World War II. All native Germans—even those who had become citizens of the United States or other countries—were classified as "aliens." Over 2,000 of these people were interned.

As the war began in Europe, Jones publicly opposed it. This stance gained notoriety as the United States was gradually drawn into the conflict. In a widely publicized speech in August 1917, he flatly stated, "All war is unchristian." For this statement, he was brought before a committee of the House of Bishops. Their first recommendation was that he be allowed to continue as bishop of Utah but discontinue his remarks against the war. However, the presiding bishop at the time, Daniel Tuttle,[1] forced a second hearing. It required of Jones that he take a leave of absence. Under the pressure of this scrutiny, Jones resigned on April 11, 1918. Portions of the speech Jones made to the House of Bishops on October 18, 1917 are apt for our discussion:

> I would appeal to my own Church on the larger ground of our claims to Catholicity. How can we ever say again that we are the Church for all men of all nations and ages, if we so

abandon the world ideal and become the willing instrument of a national government? . . . I am not blind, however, to the difficulties involved, for the active expression of the point of view that I hold is believed by some to involve disloyalty to our country. But I think a distinction must be made between loyalty to country and loyalty to any particular course of action adopted by the officers of the government. It is often necessary for citizens who love their country, because they love their country, to oppose the policy of the government.

For Jones, this stance was in accord with the Gospel as he understood it. He said,

If we are to reconcile men to God, to build up the brotherhood of the kingdom, preach love, forbearance and forgiveness, teach the ideals that are worth more than all else, rebuke evil, and stand for the good even unto death, then I do not see how it can be the duty of the church or its representatives to aid or encourage the way of war, which so obviously breaks down brotherhood, replaces love and forbearance by bitterness and wrath, sacrifices ideals to expediency, and takes the way of fear instead of that of faith. I believe that it is always the Church's duty to hold before men the way of the cross; the one way our Lord has given us for overcoming the world.[2]

The House of Bishops firmly disagreed. The same day as Jones's speech, they issued a Pastoral Letter to the whole church and the nation, which began,

Our nation is at war on behalf of justice, liberty and humanity. When these are in danger, the Church's station is at the front. When the nation has with solemn deliberation entered war, voices which have spoken for neutrality, non-resistance or pacifism are silenced. We hate war, and we shrink from its horrors, but we who enjoy the privileges of civil liberty won by the blood of our fathers must, when they are endangered, defend them at the cost of our blood. . . . Loyalty demands of every citizen unconditional consecration to the service of the nation.[3]

Jones had helped found the Fellowship of Reconciliation in the United States in 1915, following the founding of the organization in the United Kingdom a year earlier. In 1939, he and three others founded the Episcopal Pacifist Fellowship, which in 1966 became the Episcopal Peace Fellowship, which remains an active witness in The Episcopal Church. In 1940 he was the Socialist Party candidate for governor of Ohio. In 1934, The General Convention of The Episcopal Church caused a national registry to be kept "of such members of the Episcopal Church as are conscientiously unable to serve in the combatant forces of the United States." In 1988, the Convention made it clear that Episcopalians had the right to conscientious objection.[4]

Honest debate among Christians between pacifists and those supportive of some form of "just war theory" continues to this day. For our purposes, it is not so much the issue that matters, but the different approaches to the church's (and the individual Christian's) involvement in public life. So let us return to our fundamental question.

What is the responsibility of the Christian in public life, including political life? We can retrace our steps through the baptismal rite to arrive at an answer. Overall, we have come to the conclusion again and again that Christian faith is inherently social. It is a faith grounded in a covenant between God and the whole of creation, including the People of God. We know this covenant not only because of a set of rules laid out for us, but through the story of God's love for creation, a story of faithfulness and faithlessness, a story in which the People of God are called to be a light to the world. The story, of course, involves individuals and their particular relationships with God, but these individuals are always individuals-in-community. It is a story, also, in which the creation is not passively acted on by humankind, but is itself an active participant.[5]

To live this life well means the development of discernment, the capacity to turn away from what alienates us from God, from one another, from the creation, and even from our best selves. However, we do not simply turn *away*; we turn *to*. For Christians this is always a turning to Jesus Christ, the way of life he lived and for which he died. This way of life as "the way, the truth, and the life" was ratified by the resurrection and is empowered by the Holy Spirit. In living that life certain titles have traditionally been important: Lord, Savior, Messiah/Christ. These titles themselves have a social content because of their exclusivist claim, at least for those who choose to follow the One to whom they are given. If Jesus is our Lord, then none other is.

In following Jesus, once again, we do not follow a series of rules he left for us. Like his Jewish ancestors left for him, he leaves for us a story, a story that exemplifies a way of living in the world. In this way the values of the world are frequently turned upside down.

This way of hope leads to a future beyond this life, but it is also a way of living now, a way that is costly. It continues to be a way lived in covenant, in relationship with God, neighbor, and creation.

The way lived in covenant is a way marked by some broad, but very determined, values. We are never Christians who have "arrived" and whose faith is "settled." We are always learning together and we are always on the move together. Humility and honesty are watchwords for how we live life. We are committed to spreading Good News in all that we say and do. This Good News is not only news about eternal salvation and heaven, but about an absolute commitment to love of neighbor, a love which strives for peace and justice, always upholding the God-given dignity of every human person.

We can pause our review at this point and put forward a tentative summary of the Christian's responsibility in public life. It is participation—action—in common life for the common good. We participate as individuals, as members of the church, and as part of other human institutions, both formal and informal, including the institution of government. We participate with the values outlined above with the overall goal always of love of neighbor (in the practice of which we believe we are also loving God) and striving toward the common good.

In this striving, in our participation in public life, we are ruled by wisdom. This requires discerning in common what is the truth and honoring what is mystery. In doing so we acknowledge that we all are both gifted and limited. There are things we know and things we do not know. It is not that we do not seek answers to what we do not know, but that we have a profound respect for the fundamental mystery of life. This means we have a profound respect for each other despite our differences. We expect that in those differences we will be shown things we might not otherwise know, and that at least sometimes what we will be shown is the mystery of life at which we can only be in awe together.

Ultimately, we respect the longing of each one of us, and for groups of us, including nations, to simply belong. We desire to belong as people with unquestionable dignity, for whom the mystery of life and death brings a fundamental equality of experience, and who seek to offer our dignity and experience to God and one another with purpose.

One of the things this fundamental understanding means is that Christians cannot claim either to be above politics, or to be neutral. Every social act is a political act, as we have seen. But are there limits to what politics means in the church and for the Christian? I believe there are three very distinct ways of practicing politics that are, in fact, unhelpful and damaging not only to Christian community, but to community as a whole. All three fall under the banner of "partisanship."

First of all, the church as a whole should not involve itself in political parties. Individual members may do so, but even then, they should hold that membership lightly (like their attachment to anything but God). The party cannot dictate a Christian's conscience or the choices of candidates for public office or policies they support or oppose. They must risk the label of "not a good Democrat" or "Republican in name only." The Christian response to anything like these labels ought to be a demonstrative shrug.

Second, they must not use their religious conviction as a smokescreen or battering ram, to prove how right they are in the public policies or candidates they support. This is as basic as the third commandment: "You shall not make wrongful use of the name of the LORD your God, for the LORD will not acquit anyone who misuses his name."[6] One may, of course, cite one's religious convictions, but any sense of "God says this" must be avoided. This way of speaking, of course, comes naturally to some Christians, and it will feel like a restraint to avoid speaking this way. Yet that is exactly what the third commandment expects of us: restraint in speaking of or for God. That this commandment has been reduced over time as simply a prohibition against swearing using the literal name of God (or of Jesus) is very unfortunate. God's name in Jewish thought is more than a word, but a presence, at once intimate and free. "To avoid 'using the name,'" says Walter Breuggemann, "means that God's power must not be domesticated by us and for us." We cannot "enlist" God in our attempts "to have life on our own terms."[7]

Third, politics must not be a "zero-sum game" (or any other kind of game for that matter), where winners and losers are a given. Party politics tends to devolve into this way of thinking. Every issue is seen as a win-lose proposition for the party. Being on the winning side of the equation becomes the primary imperative. American journalist Robert Wright, in his 1999 book, *Non-zero: The Logic of Human Destiny*, argues that positive cultural evolution requires creating "non-zero-sumness," that is, leaving win-lose propositions behind.[8] If he is right (and I think he is), we are in a period of serious cultural devolution. That Christians are part of this devolution ought to be a major scandal. If nothing else, zero-sum thinking inevitably leads to what is arguably the greatest sin for Jesus: hypocrisy.

So, we return again to the question: What *is* the responsibility of a Christian in public life? It is first and foremost, any action which promotes the well-being of society, works for the common good, or, in the words of the Baptismal Covenant, strives for justice and peace among all people, respecting the dignity of every human person. Politics is primarily not theory or ideology; it is action. And it is action to which all of us are called. Writing in 1934, Vida Dutton Scudder, an Episcopalian educator and social reformer put it this way, with an important caveat.:

> We are the Church: you, and you, and I. . . . Now to denunciation of social evils and to the yearning for a new age, many of us yield swift assent. But when the summons to action reaches us, most of us feel perfectly helpless. We could do something while the call was confined to charity. In "the alleviation of human suffering and want" every honorable church member has probably played his part, at expense, now of money, now of time and effort. But by this more stirring call we are baffled: as to this great truth of building a new world, we do not know in concrete terms what is expected of us.[9]

The caveat is *what* action, that is, beyond "charity." Charity in this sense is not a bad thing. A weekly feeding program to combat hunger requires both monetary support and the contribution of time and physical effort. But Scudder knows this falls short of addressing the problem. Verna Dozier, a more contemporary voice in this tradition, throughout her ministry continued to ask the question, "What needs to change so that the feeding program is no longer necessary?" This is a systemic task, she said. "How do we change the system that creates people who live with hunger as a constant companion?"[10]

Both Scudder and Dozier knew the frustration of many (if not most) Christians to know what to do beyond stop-gap measures. A significant aspect of this frustration, I believe, is caused by the sense that one person cannot make a difference on such a large scale. What can I do to change the system? This brings us to a second understanding of what acting in public life means for the Christian.

Public life is just that—public—meaning any public act is an inherently social act. Something we are called to do together. In all our public acts, we must seek common ground on which to act on both large and small scales. The public life to which we are called is also participation in a process, which means that little acts do add up to make a difference. We need to educate ourselves, fearlessly. We need the honesty to which we are called by the Baptismal Covenant to know how we as a people fall short, and then how we as individuals participate in that falling short. The actions that grow out of this fearless examination of the way the status quo negatively impacts the "dignity of every human person," may at first appear to be drops in a bucket. Yet drops in the bucket do fill the bucket! Dorothy Day once said:

> One of the greatest evils of the day . . . is the sense of futility. Young people say, "What can one person do? What is the sense of our small effort?" They cannot see that we can lay one brick at a time, take one step at a time; we can be responsible only for one action of the present moment. But we can beg for an increase of love in our hearts.[11]

One important aspect of politics for the Christian is as a noble vocation. We desperately need politicians who rely on their relationship with Jesus, forged in their baptism and nurtured in their regular participation in the Eucharist. It is the Eucharist, as we have seen, that establishes the pattern, the vision of the world as God would have it, what Verna Dozier called "The Dream of God." It calls us into a community of ongoing reflection and renewal. It calls us to put our own lives on the altar, united with the life of Jesus. It makes of us Jesus's body given for the life of the world. St. Augustine, in a sermon for the Day of Pentecost, said,

> If you desire to understand the Body of Christ, listen to the apostle who tells the faithful, "Now you are the Body of Christ and its members." If, therefore, you are the Body and the members of Christ, your mystery is placed on the Lord's table; you receive your own mystery. Respond, "Amen," to what you are, and by responding give your assent. You hear, "The Body of Christ," and you respond, "Amen." Be a member of Christ's Body so that your Amen may be true.[12]

If the above is to be taken seriously, and the mystery found on the altar is to be lived out "in word and deed," one might reasonably ask whether it is possible for a Christian to be a politician, given that all but a tiny minority of politicians in the United States are members of one of two political parties? In all honesty, the answer is that it is extraordinarily difficult, along the lines of Jesus's well-known metaphor of a camel needing to go through the eye of a needle (Mark 10:25–27). Jesus is speaking of the challenge of "someone who is rich to enter the kingdom of God." The metaphor is clearly intended to signal an impossible situation, although Jesus reminds us in the passage that "for God all things are possible."[13] We can substitute "politicians" for "the rich" in this metaphor, recognizing what seems impossible—keeping Gospel values above a political party. We cannot, however, let ourselves off the hook. "For all things are possible with God," and so it must be for Christians in the public arena. Politicians who are also Christians will not have an easy time "threading the needle," of faithful political service, but they must always approach doing so as possible, and consider it a gospel imperative to do so.

The problem of politicians putting party over covenant occurs when Christian politicians are not held to Christian standards, and their adoption of particular ideologies and their dabbling with hypocrisy excused as "the way things are." The church should not dictate precise stances on particular issues to its members who are politicians, although it may certainly take positions on such issues. But the standard of the common good, the equality before God and the inherent dignity of all persons, must be the constant and consistent measure of accountability. Within that framework there might very well be differences of opinion as to the method to achieve these values. Yet the method supported must always be subject to the fundamental values, and not the other way around.

In our current political system, it is easy to imagine that a Christian living out the core values of Jesus will make a very poor politician, or at least a poor member of a political party. It is obvious, however, that we desperately need women and men of both political parties whose impulse is to raise questions and insist on conversations about what is best for the good of all. It won't do for all Christian politicians to choose to be independent of political parties (although some might well do so and perhaps more should). Political parties, like all institutions, only change from the inside.

Political debate concerning public policy will change dramatically, both within political parties and between them, when politicians see their opponents as neighbors, with whom they are bound by covenant to love and treat with the highest dignity. Can we imagine the difference it would make for the political "game" to be seen not as zero-sum, but as dignity-for-all? Imagine the politician who takes seriously St. Paul's injunction to "outdo one another in showing honor" (Romans 12:10). While it is surely true that the "what" of political policy is important, the "how" comes first. And if Christians are to positively impact public discourse, it is the "how" about which we must be clear, and for which we must hold one another accountable.

As an example, take the debate about the role of mental health in the epidemic of gun violence in the United States. The "what" is a greater attention to mental health, potentially tying mental health to gun licensure, and so-called "red flag laws" that identify individuals with mental health issues and prohibit them from gun ownership. The "how" involves the dignified treatment of those who struggle with mental health, avoiding scapegoating them as a class of people who are inherently dangerous, and protecting their right as citizens to equal protection under the law.

Bishop Paul Jones asked his fellow bishops, Christians, and citizens to choose the way of peace, that is, the way of faith rather than the way of fear. It is not always easy to know the difference between the two. It takes discernment to know which path one is on, and to what long-term results one's short-term actions can lead. Discernment is impossible without a commitment to asking questions and looking at the world with a critical eye, the very same critical eye that one is willing to train on oneself. Honesty and humility are essential.

Discernment always requires community. Too often we expect our politicians to know the answers both on their own and immediately. We criticize them if they seem indecisive. But those of us who have expectations of politicians need to be honest as well. As Rowan Williams says, "Honesty . . . has something to do with whether or not society expects in its political class a degree of self-criticism and self-questioning, or whether it continues (we continue) to project unreal expectations of problem-solving omnipotence onto its leadership."[14]

In a world of instant communication, discernment may seem like fiddling while Rome burns. Yet taking the time both to understand what is best for the common good and the best way for implementing it may be more essential to our common life than ever before. And the ability to question one's own thinking (as well as "the party-line") and to change one's mind is really the only way we have of keeping to the right path.

Our Baptismal Covenant commits us to the way of peace, and not just peace that is in our own interest. "Will you strive for justice and peace *among all people* . . .?" is the question. Ancient Israel's understanding of peace—*shalom*—was broad and deep in its meaning. *Shalom* means not only the lack of conflict between me and my neighbor, but the well-being of both me and my neighbor. We must develop the capacity to want what is best for myself/

ourselves *and* my/our neighbor(s). Developing this capacity means the willingness to act for that well-being, to do those things that cause well-being to exist now and in the future.

I said the way of peace is the way of faith rather than fear. Fear keeps us from acting faithfully: fear of the other, the unknown, the strange. Fear is overcome first and foremost by breaking down the barrier we naturally place between ourselves and the other. This means not only accepting their difference. It means understanding oneself to be the other, the unknown, the strange.

In my first parish, in the days before "cut and paste" was common place, our parish administrator typed Psalm 146 into a service leaflet, with verse seven beginning, "The LORD loves the righteous; the LORD cares for the strange," with the "r" left off that final word. The typo became a lesson for us all on its own. We are all of us "strange," and we need to approach one another with faith rather than fear, as we all share in God's love and concern. Such is the way of peace, and the way of life that triumphs over death.

CHAPTER 12

The Way of New Life

What was the point, the purpose, of my *salvation, if it did not permit me to behave with love toward others, no matter how they behaved toward me?*

—James Baldwin, *The Fire Next Time*

On the first day of January 1808, the members of the African Episcopal Church of St. Thomas gathered to celebrate a significant milestone in the history of the United States: the abolition of the African slave trade. Slavery itself had not been abolished, and would not be until the end of the Civil War and the ratification of the Thirteenth Amendment to the U.S. Constitution on December 6, 1865. But the people of St. Thomas knew that the end of the slave trade was a momentous occasion. They looked in hope for this act to be the beginning of the end.

Their rector was the Rev. Absalom Jones, who was the first person of African descent to be ordained a priest in The Episcopal Church, on September 21, 1802. The Church itself had been founded in 1792. In October 1794, after its members voted on affiliation with The Episcopal Church, St. Thomas was admitted into the Diocese of Pennsylvania, although it was not allowed clergy or lay seats at the annual Diocesan Convention (a prohibition that lasted until 1862). At the time of the first worship services at St.

Thomas, the founders and trustees issued a statement about their intent in establishing the church. It read, in part,

> to rise out of the dust and shake ourselves, and throw off that servile fear, that the habit of oppression and bondage trained us up in. And in meekness and in fear we would desire to walk in the liberty wherewith Christ has made us free. That following peace with all men, we may have our fruit unto holiness, and in the end, everlasting life.[1]

In his sermon for the celebration, Jones began with Exodus 3:7–8, in which the Lord says that he has seen the affliction of his people in Egypt, heard their cry, known their sorrows, and has come to deliver them. Jones described the plight of the people in Egypt: "All was misery, all was grief, all was despair." Yet they were not forgotten. God saw and acted. And thus God, he said, has seen the plight of those living under oppression in their own day. It is his glorious nature to do so. God acts on behalf of the oppressed, and God has "come down to deliver our suffering countrymen from the hands of their oppressors."[2]

Jones and the members of St. Thomas surely knew that all was not well, and they surely were not going to stop advocating for the end of slavery itself. But they knew that God was acting. God was making a way where there seemed to be no way. And this way God was making was inevitably headed for deliverance, for freedom. Jones himself would never see this way born out in history (he died in 1818), but that never stopped him from witnessing to it and proclaiming its inevitability. Like those described in the Letter to the Hebrews, he "died in faith without having received the promises, but from a distance [he] greeted them" (Heb. 11:13).

What Jones and the members of St. Thomas were describing, and living, was the pattern of human life attested to throughout the Bible. That life, as we have shown, is grounded in the notion of covenant, a vital biblical word that is also tied into the sacramental life of the church as it is begun in baptism. In chapter 3 we found the greatest of biblical stories behind the command of covenant—the Exodus/Sinai experience—in the "Thanksgiving over the Water" in the middle of the baptismal rite in the Book of Common Prayer. Let's return to that prayer to find this "pattern of human life" that we can see in Jones's story:

> We thank you, Father, for the water of Baptism. By it we are buried with Christ in his death. By it we share in his resurrection. Through it we are reborn by the Holy Spirit.

Christians assert there is a pattern to life, a pattern found deep in the creation itself, and, therefore, deep within the heart of God. It is the pattern of life, death, and resurrection; life, death, and new life. Jesus lived this pattern, which is one of the reasons Christians very early on began to understand that Jesus was a part of God from the beginning, really before the beginning. We express this in the Nicene Creed by saying he is, "eternally begotten of the Father . . . begotten, not made, of one Being with the Father."

We call this pattern "the Paschal Mystery." "Paschal" is not a familiar word to many. We may know it from the great candle that is lit from the new fire at the Great Vigil of Easter and burns throughout Eastertide, signifying the continued presence of the risen and ascended Christ with us. "The Paschal Candle" is one of the few objects whose use in worship is mentioned and assumed in the Book of Common Prayer. In most languages, some form of *pascha*, is used for what we in English call "Easter."[3] In Spanish, for instance, Easter is *Pascua*; in French, *Pâques*; in Swahili, *Pasaka*.

The word "paschal" is important because it is the biblical word (in both Hebrew and Greek) for "Passover," *pesach* in Hebrew, *pascha* in Greek. *Pascha* is related to the Greek word for passion or suffering, and, in English, passage. Passover, for Jews, is a celebration of the "passing over," or passage from slavery to freedom, what we know as the story of the Exodus. Specifically, it refers to the night when the angel of death sent to kill all the first-born of Egypt "passed over" the homes of the Jews who put the sign of lamb's blood on their doorposts and lintels (Exodus 12:1–20). The celebration of this feast by Jesus and his disciples forms the backdrop of the Last Supper,[4] and what became known as Jesus's passion, leading to his crucifixion. The language of the Jewish Passover was adopted by Christians to speak of both Jesus's passion and his passing over from death to life. Hence, the exchange after the breaking of bread in the Holy Eucharist in the Book of Common Prayer: "Christ our Passover is sacrificed for us: Therefore let us keep the feast" (p. 337 & 364, and see 1 Corinthians 5:7).

The prescribed use of the Paschal Candle in the prayer book is also instructive. At the end of the Exsultet at the beginning of the Easter Vigil, the rubric says, "It is customary that the Paschal Candle burn at all services from Easter Day through the Day of Pentecost." The assumption is also that the candle burns at all services that include Holy Baptism (or the reaffirmation of baptismal vows) (p. 313). It is also universal practice (and assumed by the Book of

Common Prayer, p. 467) that it burn at all services marking the death of a Christian, where it may take the place of the processional cross, leading the procession ahead of the body or remains into the church.

This use of the Paschal Candle enacts the equating of the Jewish Passover and Christ's Passover with ours. So, in the Exsultet at the Great Vigil, is sung (p. 287),

This is the night when you brought our fathers [and mothers], the children of Israel, out of bondage in Egypt, and led them through the Red Sea on dry land.

This is the night, when all who believe in Christ are delivered from the gloom of sin, and are restored to grace and holiness of life.

This is the night, when Christ broke the bonds of death and hell, and rose victorious from the grave.

The above words give us a clue about the intention of Christian life. The middle sentence is not about the Christian passage to heaven, but the rescue from sin to new life in the here and now. I love the phrase, "the gloom of sin." Sin is anything that depresses life, that oppresses life, that dims our vision. (Recall Paul's image from 1 Corinthians 13: "now we see in a mirror, dimly.") Grace is the passage from gloom to vision. We call it grace because we recognize that it is fundamentally a gift from God. The energy to make this passage is not something I can generate myself. It is only something I can learn to recognize and respond to, and in the recognition and the response comes renewal. The initiative is, however, God's.

One cannot believe in the possibility of new life, of a "new creation" in the words of St. Paul, if one does not believe that one very important thing about human beings is true: that they can change. Change (related to Christian notions of repentance and conversion) is a significant part of the life–death–new life pattern we call the Paschal Mystery.

To change almost always involves a death, a letting go, of something once assumed and often held dear. That is the human part in the act of grace, of new life. Grace is the assurance of God's love, unconditionally given. That is the easy part (although to believe that God does indeed love "unconditionally" can have its own difficulties). The hard part is to receive that grace unconditionally.

What does it mean to receive grace unconditionally? It means to accept the change—the conversion of life—that is enabled by grace. It means not to bargain with God or keep one's fingers crossed. Not to accept anything less than the change that is required of me. It is the willingness to be found by God and used by God for God's purposes. And God's purposes always point in the direction of new life. Israel's prophets were convinced of this truth:

I am about to do a new thing; now it springs forth, do you not perceive it? (Isaiah 43:19)

The days are surely coming, says the LORD, when I will make a new covenant with the house of Israel and the house of Judah. (Jeremiah 31:31)

A new heart I will give you, and a new spirit I will put within you; and I will remove from your body the heart of stone and give you a heart of flesh. (Ezekiel 36:26)

Those who were with Jesus during his earthly life quickly learned after his death that their mission had not ended, that God's purposes had not been thwarted, as it had seemed. They had experienced so much life in his presence. His death seemed to take that all away. "We had hoped," said Cleopas and his companion to the (as yet) unrecognized risen Jesus on the road to Emmaus (Luke 24:13–35). "We had hoped." They are three of the saddest words human beings can utter. Cleopas and his companion were on their way home to get on with the lives they had left behind to follow the great promise of this man. "We had hoped." Death had won. They had been fools to believe that God was doing a new thing in Jesus of Nazareth.

Of course, they found out otherwise. They recognized him in the breaking of the bread and in the remembrance of their burning hearts. When he wrote those words—"Were not our hearts burning?"—did Luke think of the passage from Ezekiel about God's desire to turn hearts of stone into hearts of flesh? We can imagine that he did.

The first followers of Jesus experienced new life, God's promise to keep doing new things, bringing new life. They still did not quite know what that meant. As Luke begins his second volume—the Acts of the Apostles—Jesus's followers desperately ask, "Lord, is this the time when you will restore the kingdom to Israel?" Whenever I read or hear that question, I always hear a heavy sigh from Jesus. They still don't quite understand, but there isn't anything more he can do. "I can't answer that question," he says. All he knows is that they "will receive power when the Hoy Spirit has come upon you; and you will be my witnesses in Jerusalem, in all Judea and Samaria, and to the ends of the earth" (Acts 1:6–8).

Then Jesus leaves them and the Gospel story of the acts of Jesus becomes the Acts of the Apostles. They will enthusiastically begin and occasionally falter. The Book of Acts is full of the pattern of the Paschal Mystery: life, death, and new life. Most famous of all is the conversion of Saul the zealous persecutor of the followers of Jesus, to Paul who will play an enormous role in the witness of the Jesus Movement "to the ends of the earth."

There are two details in Paul's conversion story that are important to our own experience of conversion. His encounter with the risen Christ—the Truth—knocks him off his horse (if you've ever fallen off a horse you know this is no small thing), and he is blinded. Letting go, accepting death, things involved in any change we face, any conversion to the truth that is necessary for us, will be a serious experience. Conversion will be disorienting, painful, and will take time. And it may very well be that we cannot complete the transformation to new life without outside help. In Paul's case it was a man named Ananias, one of those followers of "the Way" in Damascus that Saul had been on his way to "breathing threats and murder" against. Ananias restores Paul's sight *and* speaks up for him in the community, testifying that change is possible.

That change is possible is at the very heart of Christianity, but we have a great deal of trouble believing it. How many times do we hear—or think or say ourselves—that so-and-so "will never change." We use the cliché that "a leopard never changes its spots," or tell the cautionary tale of the scorpion that hitches a ride with a frog across a river and stings the frog before they get to the other side, causing both their deaths. The scorpion's last words are, "It's in my nature."

The perception that people do not change, like most human perceptions, is grounded in reality. Some people do not change. We have all seen that and experienced it. Yet that observation is not a universal constant. People can change, and most of us have also seen examples of it. Of course, the change can be for the good or it can be for the worse.

I sometimes wonder if behind the hard and fast "rule" that people cannot change is the underlying desire for things not to change in our own lives. It has always seemed to me that the vast majority of us are naturally conservative, especially those of us who live with a certain amount of privilege. For the most part, I live a very comfortable existence, and have no desire for that to change.

Change happens (or is kept from happening) on a variety of levels, a thorough description of which would require a separate volume. If one puts the word "change" into a search engine, a host of variants will come up, from simple definitions of change, websites that can help you participate in public policy change, sites in your area where you can have your oil changed, and clothing items into which you might change to gain a certain attraction!

What we are talking about is change on an affective, public, and moral level. In terms of the title of this book, it is the change required in our own way of thinking and being that can lead us to understand and take up our Christian responsibility in the world. It is the change that can lead to right action. In *The Fire Next Time*, James Baldwin demonstrates this principle:

It is the responsibility of free men to trust and celebrate what is constant—birth, struggle, and death are constant, and so is love, though we may not always think so—and to apprehend the nature of change, to be able and willing to change. I speak of change not on the surface but in the depths—change in the sense of renewal. But renewal becomes impossible if one supposes things to be constant which are not—safety, for example, or money, or power. One clings then to chimeras, by which one can only be betrayed, and the entire hope—the entire possibility—of freedom disappears.[5]

I have frequently used the word "deep" to signify our need to do more than scratch the surface of our spiritual lives, to rise to a more thoughtful and careful understanding of how the world works and answer the radical call to love our neighbors as ourselves. It is this level of change about which Baldwin speaks, and his description of what the struggle is at this level is important: the idols we construct and to which we cling (he calls them "chimeras") versus the freedom toward which one can hope.

A chimera is a mythical beast composed of many disparate parts. In Greek mythology a chimera is a female monster with a lion's head, a goat's body, and a serpent's tale, usually fire-breathing. Baldwin's use of it here is highly evocative. It is my own experience that when I discover an idol to which I cling it is hardly ever anything simple. It is almost always a mishmash of things that I have constructed over time, sometimes consciously, sometimes not. For example, if I'm clinging to money, it is actually to my parents' view of money (especially from my childhood when my family was struggling economically), my desire to be free from any kind of want, the need I have to "look good" in other people's eyes, and the desire to be generous. The parts of the chimera/idol do not all have to be negative. Positive desires can be part of an idol, and almost always are.

Yet Baldwin says these chimeras can only betray us. It is possible that for a long period of time they seem to serve us well, but they inevitably betray us because the parts together create a reality that is delusional, a bubble that is bound to burst. The delusion of reality we create will inevitably be challenged and superseded by actual reality—the truth about our lives and all human life. This truth will always prevail, even if it takes the reality of death to do so.

We cling to these chimeras, however, because we do not want to wait, and the promise of new life, of freedom given to us not on our own terms but by "a higher power," is rarely given all at once. Baldwin calls it "hope," and "possibility." Neither of these things satisfies our need for good things to happen in our life now. We do not want what the Letter to the Hebrews calls "glimpses." The writer speaks of the great heroes of the faith from Abraham onward, and admits that none of them received "the promises" of God. "From a distance they saw them and greeted them" (Heb. 11:13).

Why does God work in this way? It is a legitimate question, and one which the writer of Hebrews asked him or herself. The answer is intriguing, although not surprising given what we have been discovering throughout this book. The writer says at the end of Hebrews 11, after repeating the reality that the saints of the past had not received the promise, "God had provided something better so that they would not, *apart from us*, be made perfect" (Heb. 11:39–40). Here we have a strong biblical reference to what we mean when we say, "We are saved together." Salvation is experienced as we exercise our Christian responsibility, which is not primarily a matter of me doing something to or for you. Christian responsibility is my participation in the ongoing creation of us, that is, a good that is common for all people. We have previously called attention to Paul's admonition to "work out your own salvation in fear and trembling." The possessive pronoun "your" in the sentence is plural, as it almost always is when Paul speaks about salvation.

How does this apply specifically to the responsibility of Christians in public life? We have already spoken about the need for forgiveness and for the capacity to say "I was wrong" in public life. This fits within the pattern of the Paschal Mystery. To say "I was wrong" is more than saying simply, "I'm sorry." We often hear the latter in public life, though its sincerity is often questionable, especially when it is followed by an "explanation" of how the mistake was made, or how the original statement or act was misunderstood or "taken out of context." Worse yet is the addition, "I'm sorry *if what I said made you feel . . .*" which is never helpful since it puts the problem back on the person who was wronged.

"I was wrong," is a simple statement of fact, although its sincerity needs to be followed up by change, what Christians have called for centuries "amendment of life." It is the assumption of the Rite of Reconciliation (a.k.a. confession) in the Book of Common Prayer. It is what is implied in the directions "concerning the rite" by the words, "and has given evidence of due contrition" (p. 446). The Council of Trent (1545–63), which was the constructive part of the Roman Catholic Church's response to the Reformation, defined contrition as, "sorrow of heart and detestation of sin committed, *with the purpose of not sinning in the future.*"[6]

We live in a time when there is a higher degree of account-ability than perhaps ever before, with twenty-four hour news cycles, news outlets too many to number (many directed at niche audiences), and social media where news flies fast and far, if not always accurately. Accountability is a good thing, an essential part of what we mean by responsibility. Heightened accountability does raise questions, however, concerning the place of reconciliation and rehabilitation. In much public accountability there is clearly no hope possible for reconciliation or rehabilitation. In this atmo-sphere, Christians need to be clear about a few truths.

First, being honest about one's mistakes, the "evil [I] have done and the evil done on [my] behalf," is essential. Moreover, account-ability almost always requires a process of reconciliation that will include some form of rehabilitation and restitution. It is not always easy to apply this truth in a country that values free speech over almost everything. However, it is possible both to say that speech is free and that it is accountable.

Second, accountability, like everything else in the realm of human endeavor, can become an idol. It can easily become a weapon against one's perceived enemies used to silence them and exclude them from public life permanently. Christians need to take care here. We can never lose sight of the fact that even our enemies are human beings made in the image of God and, as such, gifted with dignity. This remains true no matter what someone has said or done. Jesus could not have been clearer: "Love your enemies and pray for those who persecute you" (Matthew 5:44).

Third, everyone deserves a chance at change, at rehabilitation, restoration, reconciliation. We say this clear-eyed. Some will refuse to change, we know that, but we must not telegraph the notion that once you have done wrong, that is the final word on you. To speak such about wrongdoers is to fall into the trap that Jesus so adamantly worked against, the labeling of individuals and groups as "sinners," who have a perpetual status as unclean and outside the acceptable people of God.

Fourth, forgiveness, reconciliation, and rehabilitation do not require us to be, for want of a better term, stupid. Child sex-offenders should rightfully have no further contact with children, for example. William Countryman says, "Forgiving an embezzler does not mean that I will promptly reappoint her to a similar position of trust." He goes on to say:

> Human generosity can seldom, if ever, be as completely open as God's generosity; but God's generosity can still represent the goal we hope to approximate. We move toward it when we aim, with hope, at building a common future rather than merely inflicting retribution. The highest virtue, for Christians, is not justice, but love. Love means holding a door open, wherever possible, to the future. If your enemy will not go through it with you, hold it open anyway. Perhaps your enemy will change.[7]

It may seem as if we have strayed from the topic of resurrection, but we have not. A former spiritual director of mine once asked me, "What would grace look like if you saw it walking down the street?" We were taking about what it meant to live a "grace-filled" life. One might ask the same question of "resurrection" or "new life." What would it look like if you saw it walking down the street? Countryman's use of the word "generosity" is one answer.

"Hospitality" is another. "Joy" is as well, but one must be cautious not to equate "joy" with demonstrable happiness. Joy is a profound consequence of being in tune with God's generosity and hospitality. I can feel that even if I am having a less than happy day. People with depression are not cut off from the feeling of joy. They may have a more authentic experience of it because they are not dependent on the feeling of happiness to get it. Unfortunately, those who suffer from mental illness of one sort or another often do not receive this understanding from the church. In the church we often project a sense of "we are the people who have their act together." Nothing could be further from the truth. In my first parish, one of the things we came to say about ourselves was, "We're all a mess here." And God loves us. And we try to love each other. And that is what resurrection looks like.

* * *

Returning to the baptismal Thanksgiving over the Water, there is one more image that we cannot ignore, and it has everything to do with the pattern of life we have been describing. The prayer concludes,

> Now sanctify this water, we pray you, by the power of your Holy Spirit, that those who are here cleansed from sin and born again may continue for ever in the risen life of Jesus Christ our Savior.

This sentence is fraught with two images that have led to many misunderstandings both about baptism and about how and why

Christians are made (and, therefore, how they are to live). The first is "cleansed from sin," conjuring notions of original sin and the old notion that unbaptized infants were not "saved" (a notion that still hangs around in popular imagination). The second is what we mean by the words "born again."

For our brief consideration of these two problematic phrases, let us remember both what precedes the images (the "how") and their goal (the "what"). We are "cleansed from sin" and "born again" *by the power of the Holy Spirit*. Which is to say not by any human-inspired agency, not as a result of any human act save for "showing up." God is doing something here, and we are just participating in what God is doing. Then there is the purpose, the goal, the "what." We are "cleansed from sin" and "born again" for the purpose of participating in the risen life of Jesus Christ.

It is true that in past iterations of the baptismal rite, "sin" was more present. The language of sin from the Thanksgiving over the Water, found well into the baptismal rite in the current book, was up front in the 1928 edition of the prayer book. The opening prayer said: "We call upon thee for *this Child* that *he*, coming to thy Holy Baptism, may receive remission of sin, by spiritual regeneration" (p. 274). The doctrine of original sin drove the impulse to baptize newborns as quickly as possible. The notion of original sin is no longer popular in much of the church, although this is largely because of its caricature, rather than its logic. At its core, original sin is simply a description of human nature. All of us sin, perhaps not as infants, but any parent will tell you it doesn't take long for sin to raise its ugly head, at least by the time "mine" becomes a child's favorite word. Some would say that rather than original sin, we are born into "original blessing." But it is not a matter of either/or, it is both/and, just like it will be throughout the natural born days of each and every one of us. Martin Luther rightly said that we are "simul justus et peccator," roughly "always saved and always a sinner." That is a large part of the mystery we must learn to respect in each other, and it means that the paschal pattern of life never ends as long as we draw breath.

"Are you born again?" is a question most Episcopalians and other sacramental Christians find inexplicable, if not annoying. We hear it as taking an image from a story in John's Gospel (John 3:1–17; and a very good story it is) and raising it to *the* expression of the Gospel. It also sounds like trying to turn a process into a singular event. The old joke about the Church of England bishop being asked by a street preacher if he is "born again" rings true for us. The bishop answers, "Sir, I have been born again; I am being born again; and I will be born again." But is there a sense in which the "born again" of the sacrament of baptism is a singular event? Yes, it is. We do not re-baptize. But what we believe is that everything said about us in baptism is both a sure and certain truth about us *and* something we appropriate and participate in our whole lives. If it were not so there would be no need of the Eucharist, much less those other five rites we call sacraments.

We can make a definitive statement: Our sacramental life is life lived in the Paschal Mystery, the pattern of life–death–new life. It is life lived both in the sure and certain experience of God's love known in Jesus, and the at-times comforting, at-times challenging mystery of the Holy Spirit who blows in, through, and around us, as the wind. This pattern of life is the pattern of our public life, our politics, our economics, our living into and sometimes pushing against cultural and social inclinations.

New life—resurrection—is not a repudiation of the past, but its transformation. There is no more powerful biblical witness to this than the presence of the wounds of crucifixion on the body of the risen Jesus, despite the clear implication that his resurrected body has undergone transformation. The disciples on the road to Emmaus do not recognize him, and, in John's Gospel, he is able to pass through walls. This truth of transformation rather than replacement is also played out sacramentally in the Eucharist. We remember a past event—the last supper of Jesus with his friends—and experience Jesus really present with us again.

The transformation carries on in us. Having been "buried with Christ" in baptism, we are raised as members of his Body. Having received his Body in the Eucharist, we are sent out to be his Body in the world.

CHAPTER 13

The Mystery of
the New People

> *It is useless to utter fervent petitions for that kingdom to be*
> *established and [God's] will to be done, unless we are willing*
> *to do something about it ourselves.*
>
> —Evelyn Underhill, *The Spiritual Life*

In the days of Julius and Priscilla, baptism was clearly about conversion. People like them underwent a substantial process of study, discernment, and building relationships until they were deemed ready to live in the mystery of being new people. By the time of their baptism, their way of life would have shown signs of change. They were also deemed trustworthy, an important matter for a community that was still not socially acceptable and occasionally in danger. Their status as slaves did not change, and slavery would remain a self-inflicted wound on the Body of Christ for nearly 2,000 years. Moreso, it would be a deep and deadly wound on the people whom the church allowed, encouraged, and in many places demanded to live in slavery. Indeed, that legacy continues in forms of institutional racism and other prejudices that still plague the church and the world.

The world around Julius and Priscilla did not change in an immediate sense, but they had changed. Their faith gave them a dignity that no status could take away from them. Archbishop Desmond Tutu famously said that the most dangerous book the practitioners of apartheid did not keep from the oppressed was the Bible. It told them they were loved and free in the eyes of God, and told a story whose primary theme was the liberation of the oppressed. This faith also existed in many enslaved people in the United States, a faith we can hear and join in the songs they sang. They sang of the great stories of the Bible as their own.

> Go down, Moses,
>
> way down in Egypt's land;
>
> tell old Pharaoh
>
> to let my people go.[1]

Our path through the rite of baptism has given us a rich language that helps us describe the change begun in Priscilla and Julius and all who have come after them: the way of turning, of honesty and humility; the way of living good news in the love of neighbor and the upholding of human dignity; the way of wisdom and belonging, of living in the household of God, as priests offering life in the pattern of Christ's life, death, and resurrection.

The world around the pair may not have changed. Their lives' effect on that world did, I have no doubt, make a difference. In a culture of power, domination, violence, oppression, and vast inequalities, their resistance to living in these ways made a difference. If nothing else, their world was a world where violence reigned. In the Christian story of which they were now a part, they saw a vivid example of that reign of violence, that is, the passion and death of Jesus. It was a passion and death that was repeated countless times when the Roman Empire felt threatened. But the mystery behind "the New People" was the resurrection, the power of life to overcome death, and of love to overcome violence.[2]

I hope I have made the case that in our own day, such resistance is as urgent for us as it was for them, and that resistance must be played out in our public lives, often by outright opposition. We sing about the old, old story of Jesus and his love, but outside our church walls that story has become thin and dim. It is thinned by those who would make Jesus into the leader of their own agenda, as a divine Captain America—the Jesus waved around at the Capitol insurrection on January 6, 2021. The story grows dimmer as those charged with telling the story become more and more anxious about the church's survival, and begin to lose touch with the story's vital importance for the sake of the world.

In a recent *Vox* podcast entitled, "Why is it so hard to forgive?" the author, Sean Illing, converses with Elizabeth Bruenig, a writer for *The Atlantic*. The podcast jumps off from a tweet Bruenig, a self-professed Christian, had written: "As a society we have absolutely no coherent story—none whatsoever—about how a person who's done wrong can atone, make amends, and retain some continuity between their life/identity before and after the mistake."[3] I admit being stunned when I read that declaration. I was having trouble thinking past it. How can anyone say this? "What about the story of Jesus?" I was stuck with that question.

I finally realized I was stuck because deep down I know she is right. Not that there is no story, but because it carries so little weight among us. The Jesus story is obscured, on the one side, by the complete denigration of that story in conservative cultural Christianity, and, on the other, by such timidity about it in liberal Christianity. The damage done to the story is reaching such a crisis point that a writer who is familiar with that story (and a believer in it) can clearly see that it has almost no impact on American public life.

One answer to this problem would be to keep it to ourselves. If all Christians would just stick to the story in their own churches and for the sake of individual spiritual gain, maybe the story could recover its former place, at least generally known and respected. It's obvious by now that I do not believe that for a moment. But neither do I believe there is an easy fix. It's tempting to say, "Just start loving people. It's all about love." That is not wrong, but the capacity to love as Jesus loves takes conversion. It takes courage and conviction—the vision of a God (to quote St. Paul) "whose power working in us can do infinitely more than we can ask or imagine" (Ephesians 3:20). Those things that are "more than we can ask or imagine" are things like honesty, forgiveness, and reconciliation.

Geoffrey Anketell Studdert-Kennedy was a priest of the Church of England and army chaplain during World War I. The things he saw in the war profoundly affected his view of the world, the church, and God. After the war he saw that the Christian story was losing its power because it had lost its focus. We are, I believe, in the same downward spiral that he saw. Studdert-Kennedy tells a powerful story in his book *The Hardest Part*. It's worth not only quoting it, but the context he gives it.

When a chaplain joins a battalion no one says a word to him about God, but every one asks him, in a thousand different ways, "What is God like?" His success or failure as a chaplain really depends upon the answer he gives by word and by deed. The answer by deed is more important, but an answer by words is inevitable, and must somehow be given.

When the question was put to me in hospital I pointed to a crucifix which hung over the officer's bed, and said, "Yes, I think I can tell you. God is like that." I wondered if it would satisfy him. It did not. He was silent for a while, looking at the crucifix, and then he turned to me, and his face was full of doubt and disappointment. "What do you mean?" he said: "God cannot be like that. God is Almighty, Maker of heaven and earth, Monarch of the world, the King of kings, the Lord of lords, Whose will sways all the world. That is a battered, wounded, bleeding figure, nailed to a cross and helpless, defeated by the world and broken in all but spirit. That is not God; it is part of God's plan: God's mysterious, repulsive, and apparently perfectly futile plan for saving the world from sin. I cannot understand the plan, and it appears to be a thoroughly bad one, because it has not saved the world from sin. It has been an accomplished fact now for nearly two thousand years, and we have sung hymns about God's victory, and yet the word is full of sin, and now there is this filthy war. . . . I tell you the Cross does not help me a bit; it makes things worse. I admire Jesus of Nazareth; I think he was splendid, as my friends at the front are splendid—splendid in their courage, patience, and unbroken spirit. But I asked you not what Jesus *was* like, but what God *is* like, God who willed his death in agony upon the cross, and Who apparently wills the wholesale slaughter in this war. Jesus Christ I know and admire, but what is God Almighty like? To me he is still the unknown God.[4]

Studdert-Kennedy then asks the reader, "How would you answer him?"

Indeed. The question was asked over a hundred years ago, but some version of the soldier's musings live on. In our day, I hear it simplified: Christianity is not especially helpful. "I just don't see why it's important or relevant," a friend of a member of our youth group said to me. "I mean, I accept that it's important to you, but what's in it for me?" You may hear self-centeredness in that question. I hear something deeper. I hear, "What difference does it make?" and if he asked the question in that way, I know he would mean what difference does it make *now*, not in some far-off heaven.

For Studdert-Kennedy and many others since him, the answer lies in the power of the cross, the cross that was the result of Jesus's public life, a life and death vindicated by the resurrection. "The Church lives on its vision of God," he wrote. "If she goes forth to meet the world armed with the vision of God upon a throne, she will die. If she goes forth in any power but the power of the cross, she will die."[5]

Prophetic? I think so.

Many committed church folk will balk at my saying that, assuming I'm saying that the cross has lost its importance for Christians. But that isn't what I mean. The cross that exists for us who still believe Jesus's story is not something with which we

desire to "meet the world" because we are unsure of its power to do
so. We have reduced it to a personal transaction about God's anger
with our individual sins, which Jesus took upon himself so that
we might live forever. We are back to our God—and our truth—
which is too small.

Kelly Brown Douglas speaks of the power of the cross in the
public square, a power to take on the violence of the world.

> The cross reflects the depth and scope of human vio-
> lence . . . the consuming violence of the world. It points
> to a world that is saturated with violence. This violence
> includes not simply the physical brutality meant to harm
> bodies, but also the systems, structures, narratives, and con-
> structs that do harm. Anything that would devalue the life
> of another is violent. . . . God responds to the violence of
> the world not in an eye-for-an-eye manner. Instead God
> responds in a way that negates and denounces the vio-
> lence that perverts and demeans the integrity of human
> creation. . . . Ironically, the non-violent power of God is
> revealed through the violence of the cross.[6]

The cross has the power of conversion when it is allowed to
meet the world, to show its place in the world, at the center of
human existence, at the heart of the whole creation. Its power
comes from the absolute solidarity God has in the human Jesus,
with you and me and the next person we meet, be they friend or
stranger, in a world obsessed with scarcity and death.

The "new people" are those who know this solidarity deep
down, who know it not only as salvation from their own madness,

but the madness of the world. The "new people" are those who know deep down that the madness of the world is their own madness and *vice versa*. Douglas quotes Audre Lord: "The true focus of revolutionary change is never merely the oppressive situations we seek to escape, but that piece of the oppressor which is implanted deep within each one of us."[7] This fundamental deep-down solidarity with all of humanity is the public witness of the cross and the politics of baptism and of public life. If we set this good news free, it will change the world. If we don't, as Paul suggests in several places, we are lost.

But what of the soldier who wanted to know what God is like, and who balked when his chaplain pointed to the cross? What do we have to say to him? It is a problem of language. The soldier spoke about the cross as part of a scheme that, in his perception, failed. The world hasn't gotten any better, he seemed to say. The cross doesn't seem to have made any real difference. The soldier was fighting in a war—as is true of most wars—in which both sides claimed God as their ultimate ally. We live in a world where this remains a devastating reality, the use (misuse) of God by opposing sides, be it in war, politics, or religious disputes. It is no wonder that so many people reject God as nonsense.

Studdert-Kennedy is right to say that our vision of God matters. He argues that the vision of God is found in the cross itself, and I agree, wholeheartedly. I also think there is something prior that is necessary for us to understand if the cross is ever going to make any sense. There is a vision we must make our own before we can grasp what the cross means for our public life.

I take my cue here from John Booty, in his understanding of the unique vision of that seminal Anglican theologian Richard

Hooker. That vision is of *wholeness*.[8] God is the embodiment of wholeness, both inwardly and outwardly. It may be said that *oneness* is the fundamental attribute of God, but it is a oneness in wholeness. This is the genius of the doctrine of the Trinity: God is one, and God is whole. God is the very experience of interdependence, mutual participation, communion. God *is* community.

When we speak either of sin or of suffering or of injustice, we speak of brokenness, all the forces that tear us apart rather than bring us together. But even the experience of brokenness is the path toward wholeness. We can only experience what it means to be whole when we first experience what it means to be broken. The cross means that God has experienced this, perhaps the most fundamental reality of human existence. The broken Jesus on the cross is God's ultimate act of solidarity with broken humanity. The resurrection is God's mysterious capacity to make things whole again, even in the midst of the ongoing brokenness of the world. Salvation is both the experience of wholeness in the present and the hope of wholeness in the future.

The story of Jesus—the whole story—must once again become worthy of our telling. We must know it so well that its rhythms become the rhythms of our life, its questions, the questions we ask, its claims about how God would have the world work, our claims about living out the dream of God; its story must become our story.

It is a time-worn sentiment that those who do not learn from history are condemned to repeat it. The Christian sentiment when it comes to the story of Jesus is actually more like this: If we do not remember the story, we are doomed *not* to repeat it.

CHAPTER 14

The Indissoluble Bond

One does not so much become a Christian as one is always in the process of becoming a Christian.

—Timothy Sedgwick, *Sacramental Ethics*

We end where we began, at a baptism in a little country church just beyond memory, dressed in the shimmer of light, in a moment that sealed a future of belonging. I have argued that this moment, in which all Christians share in some way, has deep social, political, and economic implications. Implications for a Christian's responsibility in the public square.

At the heart of baptism lies a great paradox. What is an intensely personal—and even private—event, is also a profoundly communal one. The "indissoluble bond" is forged between God and the individual and between the individual and the community of the faithful, the household of God, the New People.

There's another way of expressing this paradox. The event that marks me as different from the world around me—marked as Christ's own forever—is also an immersion in humanity as a whole, as well as the whole of creation. This paradox is easy to miss. It seems obvious that baptism makes a particular and peculiar people, with a distinctive way of being in the world. Baptism divides the world into Christians and non-Christians, does it not? Of course, it does.

The paradox is, however, that division is not the ultimate purpose of God. The separation is not God's goal; it is not God's dream. It is not God's mission for the church. The letter to the Colossians says it well, in what was most probably an early Christian hymn, rendered best in lines of poetry, and with some added emphasis.

Christ is the image of the invisible God,
  the firstborn of *all creation*;
for in him *all things* in heaven and on earth were created,
  things visible and invisible,
whether thrones or dominions or rulers or powers—
  all things have been created through him and for him.
He himself is before *all things*,
  and in him *all things* hold together.
He is the head of the body, the church;
he is the beginning, the firstborn from the dead,
  so that he might come to have first place *in everything*.
For in him *all the fullness* of God
  was pleased to dwell,
and through him God was pleased
  to reconcile to himself *all things*,
whether on earth or in heaven,
  by making peace through the blood of his cross. (1:15–20)

If Jesus is the head of the church, then the church—all the baptized—are deeply implicated in *all things*. All . . . all . . . all. And . . . and . . . and. Even the "ors" in the text have the function of "and." This is the universal, cosmic Christ as head of a universal, cosmic church whose purpose is not division but unity, wholeness. "The church," William Temple reportedly once said, "is the only society that exists for the benefit of those who are not its members."

Everything the church is called to be and do is built on the foundation of human equality. If there is a singular "Christian ethic" it is this: Love God with all that you have and love your neighbor as yourself. We call it "the summary of the law," and it is also expressed in what is called "the golden rule." Hillel the Elder, a rabbi who lived just prior to Jesus, famously put the latter this way, "That which is hateful to you, do not do to your fellow. That is the whole Torah; the rest is the explanation; go and learn."

If the Christian story and our sacramental life has any communal imperative, it is to love your neighbor as yourself. Simple, but also requiring great attentiveness, patience, and courage. The simple command demands much of us. "Love your enemies and pray for those who persecute you," Jesus said (Matthew 5:44). This command has always been difficult, and it always will be. Some might go so far as to say that it is against human nature.

It is also easy to gloss over it or to spiritualize it in such a way that it means little or nothing. "Love" can be contorted to encompass such things as judgment or prejudice, as in "love the sinner but hate the sin," a statement that is almost always applied to underscore one's feeling of moral superiority.[1] "Speaking the truth in love" (which, unlike "love the sinner but hate the sin" does appear in the Bible at Ephesians 4:15) can also be used in this prejudicial way. Rowan Williams clarifies what this saying means.

> Christians talk about "speaking the truth in love" quite a bit, but . . . this doesn't mean charitably telling people exactly where they've gone wrong. It means finding a way to speak to them that resonates with the creative word working in their depths. Love is not a feeling of goodwill toward the neighbor but the active search for that word—so that I can hear what God has to say to me and give to me through the neighbor, and also so that I can speak to what is real in the neighbor, not what suits or interests me and my agenda.[2]

Taken in the context of our current political climate, this is a radical statement. Its underlying assumption is that God's creative word is at work in every human being, whether we can see it there or not. It is our responsibility to search for it, and to maintain an openness to hearing it. I hear it said—and I have said it myself—"We have nothing to say to each other." This declaration is in truth blasphemous. It denies that God has anything to do with what you have to say. Again, there is little that is easy about this. It requires a journey of conversion, of turning away from the easy way we have of determining who is worth listening to and who is not.

Baptism sets us on a journey, a "way." It is not the way of moral superiority. It is not the way of superiority of any kind. It is the way of human equality and a commitment to the uplifting of human dignity. Baptism calls us to turn to the way of humility and simple neighborliness. Divisions and boundaries have no place in the Jesus

Movement. This includes any sense of group or national "exceptionalism." "Jesus rejects any notion of 'exceptionalism,'" writes Kelly Brown Douglas, "that may have attached to Jewish maleness. He and the Samaritan woman virtually become equals. Hence, 'the first are last and the last are first' because there is no hierarchal subordination."[3] Jesus is in solidarity with the "crucified class," by which Douglas means all those who have been judged inferior and lived in the oppressive shadow of privilege. It is not that he raises them to a new status of superiority. Rather he invites the privileged to renounce that privilege, letting go of any notion of superiority and its practical consequences. The model is Jesus's "self-emptying," or "kenosis," as described in what was another early Christian hymn, in Philippians 2.

> Christ Jesus, though he was in the form of God,
>> did not regard equality with God
>> as something to be exploited,
> but emptied himself,
>> taking the form of a slave,
>> being born in human likeness.
> And being found in human form,
>> he humbled himself
>> and became obedient to the point of death—
>> even death on a cross. (Phil. 2:6–8)

The hymn goes on to say that it is precisely for this reason—his humbling himself—that Jesus is exalted and that every tongue should confess him as Lord, to God's glory. Jesus is exalted by

186 CALLED TO ACT

servanthood, and God is glorified by this humility. These early Christian hymns show us what was essential to the earliest Christian community—the example of Jesus's solidarity with humanity and his call on his followers to live as he had lived, in a "self-emptying obedience" that valued God's presence in all things, a living example of the God who "shows no partiality."

Does this mean morality does not matter? I give the same answer as St. Paul, "By no means." The building blocks of morality need a foundation, however, and that foundation is human equality, the right for every human being to flourish, to live with dignity. It is as simple as Vida Scudder made it: "For where all are not equally matched, there is no equity and *inequality itself excludes justice.*"[4]

Is it wildly unrealistic to expect our public life to conform to the vision of our Baptismal Covenant? It is impossible to say anything but "yes." Yet if Christians and other people of faith do not seek to change the way we go about our public lives, who will? If our answer to the current political environment is to pretend we have nothing to do with it, either individually or collectively, then we not only risk ongoing stalemate, continued "culture wars," and mutual demonization, but also risk our relevance, which is already at the lowest level it has ever been.

The relevance of the church and of Christians in general is vitally important, not because we need to be culturally "with it," but because without our place as critics (as well as celebrants) in the culture, we appear to care little for the world. As Dr. King once said, "Any religion that prefers to be concerned about the souls of men and is not concerned about the slums that damn them, the economic conditions that strangle them, and the social conditions that cripple them is a spiritually moribund religion awaiting burial."[5]

* * *

The first time I remember encountering the Baptismal Covenant in the Book of Common Prayer was at The Great Vigil of Easter in 1981. I had been attending Trinity Church in my college town of Plattsburgh, New York, for about a year and a half at that point. It was also my first experience of the Great Vigil. The covenant deeply impressed me, and it was at that moment, bathed in candlelight, that I decided to seek confirmation in The Episcopal Church, which happened in the autumn of that year, on St. Luke's Day.

I was eager to share the covenant with my small group, six of us who were part of the InterVarsity Christian Fellowship at the college. We had occasional conversations about the "claim" God had on our lives, about which my fellow members who came from more evangelical traditions had much to say, but about which I was perplexed. What did God want from me? Was it some grand act of self-denial or a missionary enterprise of some sort? Was it to tell everyone I knew about the saving act of Jesus Christ on the cross? That they must be born again to be saved from hell and assured a place in heaven? I showed them the covenant from the prayer book, and said I was starting to understand what claim God had on me. There was a way of life described here about which I could get excited.

There was nothing in the covenant with which they disagreed, but they were lukewarm. A couple of them were highly suspicious of the last affirmation of the covenant, about striving for justice and peace, and upholding human dignity. Even in the early 1980s they sensed a "liberal agenda." I'll never forget one statement: "The justice thing at the end waters everything down. Respecting people's dignity doesn't save them."

I wasn't prepared to refute that criticism then, and I was still several years away from understanding the chord within me that the word "dignity" had struck. I was even more years from the revelation that truly changed my theological thinking: that in order to be saved we must be saved together. I would have thought the notion blasphemous at that early age. I would have dismissed it as some "new age" thing.

What I did not know then was that Anglicans and Episcopalians (as well as other traditions) had been saying this very thing for a long time. It actually predated the existence of Episcopalians. I wish someone had been able to show me a statement that I only recently discovered, from the House of Bishops of The Episcopal Church dating from November 9, 1933, near the beginning of the Great Depression. It is an astounding statement for its date, and even more astounding that a scant fifteen years earlier the same House of Bishops had forced Bishop Paul Jones's resignation over his pacifism. Here is a fine example of the call to Christian responsibility in the world, and a statement that has not lost its relevance ninety years later. The bishops called for "A finer type of Christian faith and courage."

No [economic] experiment which seeks to bring recovery for any one group, industrial, agricultural or any other, without considering the needs of all men, is in accord with the mind of Christ. *If we would be saved we must be saved together*, for in God's sight all human beings of whatever kindred or tongue are equally precious. The members of the church must make it clear that, as followers of the Master, they cannot give their support to any program of reconstruction which does not recognize that national recovery depends on world recovery. No mere establishment of an old economic order will suffice.[6]

"A finer type of Christian faith and courage." Indeed. Pray it may be so. Act as if it must be so.

Study Guide

You can use the questions in this study guide for individual reflection or group discussion. They are designed to connect you more deeply to the concepts in the book. The questions focus on experience and opinion rather than knowledge. There are no "right" or "wrong" answers.

After you read a question, sit with it silently for a minute, and then answer it. You might want to write down your answers.

If you are engaging in a group discussion, your group might want to adopt the Kaleidoscope Institute's "Respectful Communication Guidelines":

R—take **Responsibility** for what you say and feel without blaming others.

E—use **Empathetic** listening.

S—be **Sensitive** to differences in communication styles.

P—**Ponder** what you hear and feel before you speak.

E—**Examine** your own assumptions and perceptions.

C—keep **Confidentiality.**

T—**Trust** ambiguity because we are not here to debate who is right or wrong.[1]

Ask a volunteer to read these guidelines aloud at the beginning of each discussion session.

Your group may also want to use the Kaleidoscope Institute's "Mutual Invitation" process to ensure everyone has an equal opportunity to answer questions:

- The group facilitator asks a question and invites everyone to reflect on it for a minute.
- The group facilitator answers first.
- The group facilitator invites someone else to answer. For example, "Chris, I invite you to share your answer."
- The person invited to answer can either:
    - Briefly answer the question.
    - Say, "Please come back to me," if they want more time to think about their answer.
    - Say, "Pass," if they don't want to share an answer to the question.
- When the person has finished sharing, they invite someone else to share.
- This process continues until everyone in the group has answered the question or passed.[2]

Introduction

1. What prompted you to read this book?
2. What positive experiences have you had at the intersection of religion and public life?
3. What negative experience have you had at the intersection of religion and public life?

Chapter 1: The Indissoluble Bond

1. Where were you baptized? How old were you?
2. What was your experience of church as a child? What was your experience of church as a teen? What was your experience of church as an adult?

3. To what do you feel "rooted?"

4. Where do you feel you belong?

5. What is your opinion of politics and politicians?

Chapter 2: The Mystery of the New People

1. If you were old enough to remember your baptism, what do you recall about it? If you were not old enough to remember your baptism, what were you told about it by your parents, godparents, and others?

2. How is baptism today the same as it was in the time of Julius and Priscilla? How is it different?

3. Have you ever participated in a catechism class? What was it like?

4. Have you been confirmed? What was it like?

Chapter 3: The Way of Covenant

1. How would you explain the story of the Bible to someone who had never heard it?

2. What does the word "covenant" mean to you?

3. Which of the five baptismal promises are easy to keep and why? Which of the five baptismal promises are difficult to keep and why? (You can find the five baptismal promises in the Book of Common Prayer, on pages 304–305.)

4. How do you live out the Baptismal Covenant in your daily, public life?

5. As a Christian, how do you regard the covenant between God and the people of Israel? How do you regard Jews?

Chapter 4: The Way of Turning

1. When have you turned away from something harmful or negative and turned toward something helpful or positive?

2. What examples of evil have you encountered?

3. What does it mean for you to call Jesus Lord, Savior, and Christ?

4. From what have you been liberated or freed?

5. When have you seen political power used for evil? When have you seen political power used for good?

Chapter 5: The Way that Turns the World Upside Down

1. When you read or recite the Apostle's Creed (the Book of Common Prayer, page 96 or 304), which statements especially resonate with you and why? Which statements do you struggle to believe wholeheartedly and why?

2. What are the implications of the incarnation (God becoming a human being in the person of Jesus) to your public life?

3. What are the implications of the passion, death, and resurrection of Jesus to your public life?

4. What does "holiness" mean to you?

Chapter 6: The Way of Dignity: A Way of Good News

1. What does "dignity" mean to you?

2. When have others diminished or dismissed your dignity? When have you diminished or dismissed someone else's dignity?

3. What is your relationship to money and possessions? How do you share them with others?

4. When have you sought the forgiveness of another person? When have you forgiven someone else?

5. What, in your own words, is the "good news" of Jesus?

Chapter 7: The Way of Dignity: A Way of Reconciliation

1. To whom have you been a neighbor in their time of need? Who has been a neighbor to you in your time of need?

2. How can you be an agent of "reconciliation" in the world?

3. Who are the "enemies" you are called to love?

4. Which factional labels do you apply to yourself? Which factional labels do you apply to others?

5. What does "dignity" mean to you after reading chapters 6 and 7?

Chapter 8: The Way of Wisdom

1. What does "wisdom" mean to you?

2. Who in your life personifies wisdom?

3. How do you balance your personal rights and your social responsibilities?

4. What, in your opinion, is "the common good" and how do you contribute to it?

Chapter 9: The Way of Belonging

1. When have you felt like a valued member of a community? When have you felt alienated from or rejected by a community?

2. How is public competitiveness beneficial? How is public competitiveness harmful?

3. In what ways are you a "priest?"

4. How does your parish or congregation act like the "household of God?" How might your parish or congregation become more like the "household of God?"

Chapter 10: The Way of Communion

1. How did you feel during the COVID-19 pandemic when you could not attend church physically or receive communion?

2. How does the Eucharist benefit you individually? How does the Eucharist benefit the church collectively?

3. In your experience, how does the Eucharist empower you to be an agent for change in the world?

Chapter 11: The Way of Peace

1. Are you a pacifist, or do you believe violence is sometimes morally justified?

2. How do you participate in "common life for the common good?"

3. Are you registered to vote? Why or why not? Do you vote in every election? Why or why not?

4. With which political party are you affiliated? How do you regard and interact with people of other political parties?

5. How can you help others find common ground in our polarized society?

Chapter 12: The Way of New Life

1. How have you witnessed "new life" in yourself and others?
2. To what "chimeras" do you cling?
3. When have your taken responsibility for being wrong?
4. How have you treated those who took responsibility for their wrongs?
5. How would you answer if someone asked if you were "born again?"

Chapter 13: The Mystery of the New People

1. How have you changed during your faith journey?
2. What is your vision of God?
3. What does "the power of the cross" mean for you and your public life?

Chapter 14: The Indissoluble Bond

1. How do you love God?
2. How do you love your neighbor as yourself?
3. What needs to change in our culture? How can you help bring about that change?
4. What does "salvation" mean to you? Has this changed after reading this book?

Acknowledgments

There are many, many people who have been and are a part of my story, and, therefore, have a profound effect on it. Chief among them is my husband, chief supporter, *and* critic, John Clinton Bradley. I am blessed to also have him as a collaborator in ministry. The Study Guide in the back of this book is largely his work.

The people of the congregations I have served have shaped who I am, both as a priest and as a Christian, chief among them St. George's Church, Glenn Dale, Maryland, in the Episcopal Diocese of Washington, and The Church of St. Luke and St. Simon Cyrene, Rochester, New York. These days I serve as Priest-in-Residence at St. Thomas's Church in Bath, New York, where I can be found most Sundays teaching Sunday School in the Godly Play method. The children I have served have helped me become a better person of faith. I owe special thanks to the rector, the Rev. Dr. Melanie Duguid-May, who is also Professor of Theology, Colgate Rochester Crozier Divinity School, for her suggestions that have greatly improved this work, and for the weekly Book Group at St. Thomas's Church who read the draft. Their discussion was also vitally important. My current bishop, the Rt. Rev. Stephen Lane, has also been a great help and encouragement.

In addition to my parishes, I have been privileged to serve with colleagues—lay and ordained—who are about God's work in the world. I especially think of those who make up the Consultation, an umbrella group for the independent peace and justice ministries of The Episcopal Church, and those who worked together as the collaborative Claiming the Blessing, and especially my dear friend Susan Russell. Together we acted, in season and out of season, for the betterment of the church and the world.

My teachers and mentors through the years have had a tremendous impact on my view of faith and the world. Especially in relation to baptism and the demand of faith in action in the world, I mention Louis Weil, Leonel Mitchell, Jane Holmes Dixon, Barbara Harris, Gene Robinson, Elizabeth Johnson, David Power, and my dear friend of blessed memory Verna Dozier. I am also grateful for my creative writing teachers: Susanne Antonetta, Lauren Winner, and Scott Cairns. There are many, many others, for whom I am grateful to God.

I cannot say enough about the help and encouragement I received from my editor at Church Publishing, Eve Strillacci. Her enthusiasm for this project and her wise counsel in the editing process were an essential part of any success it has.

Lent 2023
Hornell, New York

Notes

Introduction

1. Pope Francis, *Fratelli Tutti* (2020), para. 176, https://www.vatican.va/content/francesco/en/encyclicals/documents/papa-francesco_20201003_enciclica-fratelli-tutti.html. Accessed April 17, 2023.

Chapter 1: The Indissoluble Bond

1. Allan Gurganus, *Oldest Living Confederate Widow Tells All* (New York: Alfred Knopf, 1989), 274.
2. *The Book of Common Prayer* (New York: Church Publishing, 1979), 298.
3. This quotation has long been attributed to Rowan Williams and was used frequently by Presiding Bishop Frank Griswold. I have been unable to find the source of it.
4. *The Book of Common Prayer*, 298.
5. Information from the website of The Episcopal Church: https://www.episcopalchurch.org/church-that-looks-and-acts-like-jesus/. Accessed February 12, 2023.

Chapter 2: The Mystery of the New People

1. Anonymous, *The So-called Letter to Diognetus*, trans. & ed. Eugene R. Fairweather, in *The Library of Christian Classics, vol. I, Early Christian Fathers*, ed. Cyril C. Richardson (Philadelphia: Westminster Press, 1953), 213–214.
2. It is important here to acknowledge the profound difference between "race" as an archaic construct and our contemporary use of the term. At the time of *The Letter to Diognetus* (and for many centuries afterward) "race" primarily indicated shared culture, vocation, or belief system. It was not until the seventeenth century that race was used to classify common physical traits or ancestral heritage. This use is generally understood to have begun with the publication of "A New Division of the Earth" by Francois Bernier in 1684, in which he divided the world into four or five species or races based completely on physical traits.
3. *Diognetus*, 218.

4. *Diognetus*, 220–221.

5. *Diognetus*, 221.

6. See Justin Martyr, *Writings of Justin Martyr*, eds. Alexander Roberts and James Donaldson (Houston: Veritatis Splendor, 2014), 65.

7. This is language from the *Acts of Thomas* 27, a Syriac text from the third century. This first anointing in the West became an exorcism, but this was not the case in the East. *Acts of Thomas* can be found in Lawrence J. Johnson, *Worship in the Early Church: An Anthology of Historical Sources* (Collegeville, MN: Liturgical Press, 2009), 240–243.

8. Again, language from the *Acts of Thomas* 132.

9. *Acts of Thomas* 50, 133, 158.

Chapter 3: The Way of Covenant

1. We are beginning to re-experience this dynamic as fewer and fewer people are born into Christian faith and as a cultural assumption it is fading (in varying degrees depending on where in the country or world you live). But we are still a long way from the experiences of these early converts.

2. The evidence suggests that by the time of Julius and Priscilla, the Gospels were in more or less their final form and what were considered to be Paul's letters (13 in number) were largely accepted as authoritative. However, it would be another two hundred and fifty years before the New Testament canon was settled and closed.

3. Walter Brueggemann, *Reverberations of Faith: A Theological Handbook of Old Testament Themes* (Louisville: Westminster John Knox Press, 2002), 39.

4. Walter Brueggemann, *Theology of the Old Testament: Testimony, Dispute, Advocacy* (Minneapolis: Augsburg Fortress, 1997), 420.

5. Brueggemann, *Theology of the Old Testament*, 421 & 423. Emphasis is in the text.

6. Walter Brueggemann, *Sabbath as Resistance: Saying NO to the Culture of Now* (Louisville: Westminster John Knox Press, 2014), 30. Emphasis is in the text.

Chapter 4: The Way of Turning

1. "The Shakers" is the common name of The United Society of Believers in Christ's Second Appearing, founded in the mid-eighteenth century.

Their first colonial American community was formed at Watervliet, NY in 1774. The movement's height came in the 1840's. One community—Sabbathday Lake in Maine—survives with two members today.

2. From a video link on the home page of the Sabbathday Lake website: www.maineshakers.com. Accessed October 7, 2021.

3. An example is Psalm 109:6 (NRSV): "They say, 'Appoint a wicked man against him; let an accuser (sâtân) stand on his right.'"

4. "Devil" is the common English translation of the Greek word *diabolos*, also meaning "accuser." In the temptation stories Mark uses "Satan," Luke uses "the devil," and Matthew uses both.

5. *Enriching Our Worship 1* (New York: Church Publishing, 1998), 56.

6. Walter Wink, *Engaging the Powers: Discernment and Resistance in a World of Domination* (Minneapolis: Fortress, 1992), 48.

7. Wink, *Engaging the Powers*, 67.

8. For instance, of the 157 possible Collects of the Day (the opening prayer for the Eucharist) in *The Book of Common Prayer*, 78, or 50 percent, of them use the attribute "almighty" or attribute "power" to God. (See pp. 211–251).

9. The Collect for Proper 21, The *Book of Common Prayer*, 234.

10. Luke uses "Savior" in this context in the songs of Mary (1:47), Zechariah (1:69), and the angels in their announcement to the Shepherds (2:11).

11. Edward Schillebeeckx, *Christ: The Experience of Jesus as Lord*, trans. John Bowden (New York: Crossroad, 1983), 19.

12. Eugene H. Peterson, *Christ Plays in Ten Thousand Places: A Conversation in Spiritual Theology* (Grand Rapids, MI: Wm. B. Eerdmans Publishing, 2005), 42.

13. Richard Rohr, *Everything Belongs: The Gift of Contemplative Prayer* (New York: Crossroad, 2003), 179. The emphasis is in the original.

14. Wink, *Engaging the Powers*, 62.

15. William Stringfellow, *Instead of Death* (New York: Seabury Press, 1963), 57.

16. Henri Nouwen, *Life of the Beloved: Spiritual Living in a Secular World* (New York: Crossroad, 1992), 134–135.

Chapter 5: The Way that Turns the World Upside Down

1. *The Book of Common Prayer* (New York: Church Pension Fund, 1928), 276–277.

2. Paul F. Bradshaw, *Apostolic Tradition: A New Commentary* (Collegeville, MN: Liturgical Press, 2023), 72–75.

3. Matthew 21:12–13, Mark 11:15–18, Luke 19:45–46, John 2:13–17. John differs on the timing of the incident, but the description is the same as the synoptics.

4. William Stringfellow, *Free in Obedience* (New York: Seabury Press, 1964), 50. Emphasis is in the original text.

5. Thomas Merton, *Spiritual Direction & Meditation* (Collegeville, MN: Liturgical Press, 1987), 94. Emphasis is in the original.

6. Each of these (except for Tawney) has a day of commemoration on the Episcopal Church's calendar: Maurice (April 1), Gore (January 14), Scudder (October 10), Morgan (February 26), and Temple (November 6).

7. Care must be taken in understanding the word "socialism" in this context. It is a high regard for human life and dignity, and the church's responsibility to act on behalf of this dignity. Most of the Christian Socialists eschewed party politics.

8. For an analysis of men such as Stuart and Mill and their long-term effect on American life see, Joel Edward Goza, *America's Unholy Ghosts: The Racist Roots of Our Faith and Politics* (Eugene, OR: Cascade Books, 2019).

9. Philip Turner, *Christian Socialism: The Promise of an Almost Forgotten Tradition* (Eugene, OR: Wipf & Stock, 2021), 20.

10. Frederick Denison Maurice, *The Kingdom of Christ* (Nashotah, WI: Nashotah House Reprint, 2013). First published in 1838. Quoted by Turner, *Christian Socialism*, 21–22.

11. Peter Waddell, *Charles Gore: Radical Anglican* (Norwich, UK: Canterbury Press, 2014), 111.

12. Recalled as a personal dictum in "Letter from the Archbishop of the West Indies" in *Theology* 59 (1956).

13. William Stringfellow, *Dissenter in a Great Society: A Christian View of America in Crisis* (Eugene, OR: Wipf & Stock, 2005), 159. Originally published in 1966.

14. Stringfellow, *Free in Obedience*, 16.

15. Arthur Lichtenberger, "Mutually Encouraged in Joy and Hope," in *The Day Is at Hand* (New York: Seabury Press, 1964), 121.

16. William Stringfellow, *A Public and a Private Faith* (Grand Rapids, MI: Eerdmans Publishing, 1962),65.

17. See Leviticus 19:2 and its use in Matthew 5:48 (with the unfortunate typical translation of "perfect") and Luke 6:36 where the typical translation is "merciful."

Chapter 6: The Way of Dignity: A Way of Good News

1. Brian A. Wren, *The Hymnal 1982* (New York: Church Publishing, 1985), #304. Text is copyright © 1971 Hope Publishing Co., Carol Stream, IL 60188.

2. You can learn more about this ministry at https://tlayf.com/mcc-kampala/.

3. Turner, *Christian Socialism*, 123.

4. It is Matthew (6:10) who elaborates this sentence of the Lord's Prayer to the familiar "Your kingdom come. Your will be done, on earth as it is in heaven."

5. Luke Timothy Johnson, *The Acts of the Apostles* (*Sacra Pagina* series) (Collegeville, MN: Liturgical Press, 1992), 61. The table is my arrangement of his material.

6. See Leviticus 25.

7. William Temple, *Christianity & Social Order* (London: Shepheard-Walwyn, 1976), 37. The book was first published in 1942.

8. See also 1 Corinthians 12:13 and Colossians 3:9–11.

9. John Booty, *Reflections on the Theology of Richard Hooker: An Elizabethan Addresses Modern Anglicanism* (Sewanee, TN: University of the South Press, 1998), 177.

10. Booty, *Richard Hooker*, 173.

11. Stringfellow, *Public and Private Faith*, 57.

12. Wink, *Engaging the Powers*, 89.

13. L. William Countryman, *Good News of Jesus: Reintroducing the Gospel* (Valley Forge, PA: Trinity Press, 1993), 50.

14. Countrymann, *Good News*, 48.

15. Scudder, *Social Teachings of the Christian Year*, 82.

16. The conference is called "Lambeth," after the name of the archbishop's residence in London, where the conference took place in its early days in the nineteenth century.

17. An account of my experience with this conference can be found in Peter Francis, ed., *Rebuilding Communion: Who Pays the Price* (Hawarden, UK: Monad Press, 2008), 61–66.

18. 1998 Lambeth Resolution 1.10, *The Lambeth Daily*, Thursday, August 6, 1998, p. 3. The resolution and supporting documents can be found at www.anglicancommunion.org/resources/document-library.aspx? subject=Human+sexuality&page=2. Accessed August 27, 2021.

19. Edward Schillebeeckx, *Church: The Human Story of God* (New York: Crossroad, 1990), 183–184.

20. Douglas, *Stand Your Ground*, 149–154.

21. Elizabeth A. Johnson, *She Who Is: The Mystery of God in Feminist Theological Discourse* (New York: Crossroad, 1992), 17.

22. The quote "full and equal claim …" is from Resolution A069 of the 1976 General Convention of the Episcopal Church, https://www.episcopal archives.org/cgi-bin/acts/acts_resolution.pl?resolution=1976-A069.

23. Lauren F. Winner, *The Dangers of Christian Practice: On Wayward Gifts, Characteristic Damage, and Sin* (New Haven: Yale University Press, 2018), 3.

24. Winner, *Dangers*, 95–135.

25. Stringfellow, *Public and Private Faith*, 78.

Chapter 7: The Way of Dignity: A Way of Reconciliation

1. Deuteronomy 6:5 does not include the phrase "with all your mind." The origin of this addition is not clear, but it is clearly embraced by Matthew (22:37), Mark (12:28), and Luke when they present the summary. In Matthew's version, "with all your mind" takes the place of "with all your strength/power." Luke collapses the two commandments into one, while Matthew and Mark list them as first and second.

2. See also Jesus's interaction with a Samaritan woman in John 4.

3. Dorothy Day, quoted in Plough Publishing House, "The Mystery of the Poor," *Bread and Wine: Readings for Lent and Easter* (Maryknoll, NY: Orbis Books, 2005), 315, 317.

4. Many contemporary interpreters see the larger question in this scene to be how the Gentiles (i.e., "the nations") treat Christians. See, for example, Daniel J. Harrington, S.J., *The Gospel of Matthew* (*Sacra Pagina* series), (Collegeville, MN: Liturgical Press, 1991), 355–360. While I suspect the narrower interpretation is correct as to the passage's original intention,

its application to all people is so widely traditional that I believe it has authority as such.

5. Frank Tracy Griswold III, sermon preached at the Washington National Cathedral, January 11, 2004, text found at https://www.episcopal church.org/pbfrankgriswold/sermon-at-the-service-of-investiture-of -the-xxv-presiding-bishop/. Accessed April 14, 2023.

6. Richard Hooker, *Sermon on the Nature of Pride*, found at https://www .bartleby.com/209/179.html. Accessed September 20, 2022. See also Philip Secour, *The Sermons of Richard Hooker* (London: SPCK, 2001), 87.

7. These latter words and the previous quotes are from the catechism of *The Book of Common Prayer*, 855.

8. Allan Aubrey Boesak and Curtiss Paul DeYoung, *Radical Reconciliation: Beyond Political Pietism and Christian Quietism* (Maryknoll, NY: Orbis Books, 2012), 154. The book contains an important critique of the Truth and Reconciliation process in South Africa after the fall of apartheid. Archbishop Desmond Tutu, the subject of a portion of that critique, writes a very helpful foreword to the book.

9. Verna Dozier, *Confronted by God: The Essential Verna Dozier*, eds. Cynthia L. Shattuck and Fredrica Harris Thompsett (New York: Seabury Books, 2006), 61.

10. *The New Oxford Annotated Bible of the New Revised Standard Version*, 5th ed., describes the wisdom literature of the Old Testament to be "works that focus or reflect on universal human concerns, especially the understanding of individual experiences and the maintenance of ordered relationships that lead to both success on the human plane and to divine approval. The biblical books that are generally considered wisdom literature are certain of the psalms, Job, Proverbs, and Ecclesiastes, and the apocryphal books of Wisdom, Sirach (also known as Ecclesiasticus)."

11. This is often referred to as "tribalism," which is a troubling metaphor, in that living in tribes is the normal way of ordering society for indigenous people throughout the world, including North America. The difference between tribes in these cultures is hardly ever hostile, much less a division between friends and enemies.

12. The Farewell Address can be found at https://en.wikisource.org/wiki /Washington%27s_Farewell_Address. It is worth quoting the following passage: "All obstructions to the execution of the Laws, all combinations and associations, under whatever plausible character, with the real design to direct, control, counteract, or awe the regular deliberation and action of

the constituted authorities, are destructive of this fundamental principle, and of fatal tendency. They serve to organize faction, to give it an artificial and extraordinary force; to put, in the place of the delegated will of the nation, the will of a party, often a small but artful and enterprising minority of the community; and, according to the alternate triumphs of different parties, to make the public administration the mirror of the ill-concerted and incongruous projects of faction, rather than the organ of consistent and wholesome plans digested by common counsels, and modified by mutual interests. However, combinations or associations of the above description may now and then answer popular ends, they are likely, in the course of time and things, to become potent engines, by which cunning, ambitious, and unprincipled men will be enabled to subvert the power of the people, and to usurp for themselves the reins of government; destroying afterwards the very engines, which have lifted them to unjust dominion."

13. Wink, *Engaging the Powers*, 263, 273.

14. Rohr, *Everything Belongs*, 173.

15. Wink, *Engaging the Powers*, 268.

16. The difference comes out in English translations. King James Version has Deut. 18:13: "Thou shalt be perfect with the Lord thy God." The New Revised Standard Version has: "You must remain completely loyal to the Lord your God" (Deut. 18:13).

17. This difference in Creedal language, often referred to as the *filioque* ("of the son") controversy is one of the great divisions between the churches of the East and West. It was a significant theological expression of the Great Schism of 1054 ce, a schism between Eastern and Western Christianity that has yet to be healed. The Anglican Communion committed itself at the Lambeth Conference of 1978 to remove the *filioque* clause from any future editions of the Book of Common Prayer. Follow through on this commitment has been spotty. The Episcopal Church committed itself in 1994 to drop the *filioque*, and the alternative rites in *Enriching Our Worship 1* do so (see p. 53).

18. Thomas Aquinas, *De Potencia* (Westminster, MD: Newman Press, 1952), q. 7, a. 5; cited in Johnson, *She Who Is*, 45.

19. Johnson, *She Who Is*, 229.

20. Johnson, *She Who Is*, 228.

21. Athanasius, *On the Incarnation*, trans. Archibald Robertson, in *Library of Christian Classics: Christology of the Later Fathers*, ed. Edward Rochie Hardy (Philadelphia: Westminster Press, 1954), 107.

22. Desmond Mpilo Tutu, *No Future Without Forgiveness* (New York: Doubleday, 1999), 31.

23. Temple, *Christianity and Social Order*, 67–68. Emphasis is in the original.

24. Jürgen Moltmann, *On Human Dignity: Political Theology and Ethics*, trans. M. Douglas Meeks (Minneapolis: Fortress Press, 1994), chap. 3, Kindle 444.

25. Johnson, *She Who Is*, 30.

Chapter 8: The Way of Wisdom

1. This blessing of chrism can occur if the bishop is present at the baptism, or at some previous time (often during Holy Week) and distributed to the parishes. Chrism is olive oil mixed with aromatic spices, especially oil of balsam. See *The Book of Common Prayer*, 307.

2. *The Book of Common Prayer*, 308.

3. "Wisdom" was used in the 1928 version of this prayer, which was the prayer said by the bishop immediately before the laying on of hands in Confirmation, see the 1928 version, 297.

4. Brueggemann, *Reverberations of Faith*, 232.

5. Evelyn Underhill, *The Spiritual Life: Four Broadcast Talks* (Mansfield, CT: Martino Publishing, 2013), 26. The talks were originally broadcast in 1936.

6. Temple, *Social Order*, 68.

7. Temple, *Social Order*, 69–71.

8. Temple, *Social Order*, 73.

9. Ratification of the Declaration came on December 10, 1948 (now observed as Human Rights Day) during the third session of the United Nations, meeting in Paris. Eleanor Roosevelt, former first lady of the United States and an Episcopalian, chaired the committee that proposed it. It can be found at www.un.org/en/about-us/universal-declaration-of-human-rights.

10. Rowan Williams, *Where God Happens: Discovering Christ in One Another* (Boston: Shambhala Publications, 2005). 24. Emphasis in the original.

11. Irenaeus of Lyons, *Against Heresies* 4:20.7. The full phrase is *Gloria enim Dei vivens homo, vita autem hominis visio Dei*, which I translate as "Indeed the glory of God is the living human, and the life of a human being is the vision of God." An alternative to the second part of the quote would be "and the life of a human being is the beholding of God."

12. *Letter to Diognetus*, 221.

13. St. Ambrose, *De Nabuthae: A Commentary, with an Introduction and Translation*, trans. Martin R.P. Maguire (Washington: The Catholic University of America, 1927), 83. I edited this quote for inclusive language and to make clearer what was a double negative in the original.

14. Translation of Revelation 5:9–10 from *Enriching Our Worship 1*, Canticle 18, "A Song to the Lamb," 28–29.

15. J. B. Phillips, *Your God Is Too Small: A Guide for Believers and Skeptics Alike* (New York: Simon & Schuster, 2004). Originally published in 1952. Phillips was an Anglican priest and scholar, best known for his translation of the New Testament.

16. Rowan Williams, *The Way of St. Benedict* (London: Bloomsbury Continuum, 2020), 21.

17. Williams, *St. Benedict*, 30.

Chapter 9: The Way of Belonging

1. The word "stewardship" is not found in the New Revised Standard Version of the Bible, but the term "steward" is frequently used for the household manager. See Luke 8:3; John 2:18–19; 1 Corinthians 4:1–2; and 1 Peter 4:10. The King James Version does use the word "stewardship" in Luke 16:2–4 (where the NRSV uses the word "management").

2. This optional offertory sentence is from the 1928 version of *The Book of Common Prayer*, 73. Although not in the current version, it is still widely used. Its basis is a prayer of King David at the end of his life (1 Chron. 29:14).

3. Williams, *Rule of St. Benedict*, 59.

4. Williams, *Rule of St. Benedict*, 74.

5. Williams, *Where God Happens*, 26.

6. *The Book of Common Prayer*, 306.

7. The image of Jesus as an eternal high priest is limited to the Letter to the Hebrews. It is not an image Jesus used for himself, and St. Paul never uses the title in his letters.

8. L. William Countryman, *Living on the Border of the Holy: Renewing the Priesthood of All* (Harrisburg, PA: Morehouse Publishing, 1999), 57.

9. The image is also used in Revelation 5:9–10, although the NRSV translates it as "You have made them a kingdom and priests serving our God." But see the canticle *Dignus Es* in *The Book of Common Prayer* (93–94),

which has "a kingdom of priests," and the same canticle in *Enriching Our Worship 1* (28) has "a royal priesthood."

10. Jeffrey Rowthorn, "Lord you give the great commission," found at #528 in *The Hymnal 1982* (New York: Church Publishing, 1985). The text is the third verse.

11. Underhill, *The Spiritual Life*, 29–30.

12. Underhill, *The Spiritual Life*, 28.

13. Edward Schillebeeckx, *Jesus in Western Culture: Mysticism, Ethics, and Politics* (London: SCM Press, 1987), 25.

14. Schillebeeckx, *Jesus in Western Culture*, 23.

15. Schillebeeckx, *Jesus in Western Culture*, 27.

16. Matthew 20:24–28; Mark 10:41–45; Luke 22:24–30. Luke 9:46 reports the dispute also, but in that case, Jesus takes a little child as the example of how the least among them was the greatest.

17. Peter Selby, *BeLonging: Challenge to a Tribal Church* (London: SPCK, 1991), 2–3.

18. Kelly Brown Douglas, *Stand Your Ground: Black Bodies and the Justice of God* (Maryknoll, NY: Orbis, 2015), 194.

Chapter 10: The Way of Communion

1. I am not going to enter the conversation about the validity of various attempts to get the Eucharist to individuals, such as celebrating the Eucharist without a physical congregation or drive through reception of pre-consecrated elements.

2. *The Book of Common Prayer*, 13.

3. Anthony R. Lusvardi, SJ, "Spiritual Communion or Desire for Communion? Sacraments and Their Substitutes in the Time of COVID-19," *Worship* 96, (April 2022): 161–177.

4. Annie Dillard, *Teaching a Stone to Talk: Expeditions and Encounters* (New York: Harper & Row, 1982), 40–41.

5. The common phrase "making or made my communion" is thankfully falling into disuse.

6. Winner, *Dangers of Christian Practice*, 19–33.

7. Winner, 28–29.

8. Information found at https://www.pewforum.org/2021/12/14/about-three-in-ten-u-s-adults-are-now-religiously-unaffiliated/. Accessed November 17, 2021.

9. I use the term "liberal" loosely, in a classical sense of "open-hearted." For example, the hymn "Awake, arise, lift up your voice" whose third verse reads "those hands of liberal love indeed in infinite degree." I understand The Episcopal Church to fit into this category. I also know some would disagree. And I also know many would eschew the adjective because of its current association with a particular political party and its policies. It's a word, like politics itself, that I am not willing to give up.

10. Gregory Dix, *The Shape of the Liturgy* (London: Adam & Charles Black, 1945), 744.

Chapter 11: The Way of Peace

1. Tuttle had previously served as missionary bishop of Utah (along with Montana and Idaho). He was elected bishop of Missouri in 1886. From 1903 to 1923 he was also presiding bishop. These were the days when the presiding bishop was simply the senior-most bishop in the House of Bishops.

2. Paul Jones, "Statement by Bishop Paul Jones on October 18, 1917," in *Documents of Witness: A History of the Episcopal Church 1782–1985*, ed. Don S. Armentrout and Robert Bloak Stocum, (New York: Church Publishing, 1994), 340–341.

3. "House of Bishops, Pastoral Letter, October 18, 1917," in Armentrout and Stocum, *Documents of Witness*, 342.

4. General Convention, Journal of the General Convention of The Episcopal Church, Detroit, 1988 (New York: Church Publishing, 1989), 275.

5. There are many examples of the creation as active participant. One of my favorites is Revelation 12:16. The dragon is pursuing the "woman clothed with the sun." Verse 16 begins, "And the earth (*gai*) came to the help of the woman ..."

6. Exodus 20:7; Deuteronomy 5:11. In some ordering of the commandments, especially in Roman Catholic and Lutheran churches, this is the second commandment.

7. Walter Brueggemann, "The Commandments and Liberated, Liberating Bonding," in *Interpretation and Obedience: From Faithful Reading to Faithful Living* (Minneapolis: Augsburg Fortress, 1991), 149.

8. Robert Wright, *Non-zero: The Logic of Human Destiny* (New York: Pantheon Books, 1999). Gleaned from Simon Conway Morris, "Where are we headed? Robert Wright argues that human history does indeed have a purpose," *New York Times* (New York), Jan. 30, 2000. Accessed January 31,

2022. https://archive.nytimes.com/www.nytimes.com/books/00/01/30/reviews/000130.30conwayt.html

9. Vida Scudder, "Social Problems Facing the Church in 1934," in Armentrout and Slocum, *Documents of Witness*, 358. Scudder was reacting to a Pastoral Letter from the House of Bishops (see chapter 12, below).

10. These quotes are remembrances of the author.

11. Dorothy Day, *Loaves and Fishes* (Maryknoll, NY: Orbis Books, 1997), 176.

12. Augustine of Hippo, "Sermon 272," from *Patrologia Latina*, trans. Lawrence J. Johnson, in *Worship in the Early Church: An Anthology of Historical Sources*, vol. 3 (Collegeville, MN: Liturgical Press, 2009), 77.

13. There have been many attempts to blunt the metaphor, such as making it a reference to a gate into Jerusalem called "The Eye of the Needle." There was no such gate.

14. Williams, *Rule of St. Benedict*, 37.

Chapter 12: The Way of New Life

1. "The Causes and Motives for Establishing St. Thomas's African Church . . ." in *Annals of the First African Church in the United States of America now Styled the African Episcopal Church of St. Thomas, Philadelphia*, by the Rev. William Douglas (Philadelphia: King & Baird Printers, 1862), found at www.pbs.org/wgbh/aia/part3/3 h 15t.html. Accessed March 1, 2023.

2. Absalom Jones, "A Thanksgiving Sermon, January 1, 1808," in Armentrout & Slocum, *Documents of Witness*, 181–186.

3. The word "Easter" may be derived from Eostre, the Anglo-Saxon goddess of spring and fertility. This was the Venerable Bede's position in the eighth century. More recently, some scholars have traced the word to the Latin *in albis*, the plural of *alba*, "dawn," which came through Old High German as *eostarum*. In German, Easter is *Ostern*. See Hans J. Hillerbrand, "Easter," britannica.com, Encyclopedia Britannica, October 6, 2022, https://www.britannica.com/topic/Easter-holiday. Accessed February 27, 2023.

4. The Gospels of Matthew, Mark, and Luke clearly tell the story of the Last Supper as a Passover meal. The Gospel of John says that Jesus was crucified on "the Day of Preparation," that is, the day before Passover began (hence the urgency to take the bodies down from the crosses before sundown, when the Passover would begin—presumably it was not just the weekly Sabbath, but a Sabbath "of great solemnity" (John 19:31).

5. James Baldwin, *The Fire Next Time*, in *Baldwin: Collected Essays*, ed. Toni Morrison (New York: Library of America, 1998), 339.

6. Council of Trent, session 14, cap. 4, quoted in "contrition" in *The Oxford Dictionary of the Christian Church*, 3rd ed., ed. Frank Leslie Cross and Elizabeth. A. Livingstone (Oxford, UK: Oxford University Press, 1997), 412. Emphasis mine.

7. Countryman, *Good News of Jesus*, 50.

Chapter 13: The Mystery of the New People

1. *Lift Every Voice and Sing II: An African American Hymnal* (New York: Church Publishing, 1993), #228.

2. See a helpful discussion on violence and the cross in Boesak and DeYoung, *Radical Reconciliation*, 36–37.

3. Sean Illing, "Why is it so hard to forgive? Elizabeth Bruenig on forgiveness and the performative cruelty of the digital age," *Vox*, July 12, 2021. https://www.vox.com/vox-conversations-podcast/2021/7/12/22379647/vox-conversations-elizabeth-bruenig-forgiveness-social-media. Accessed March 18, 2022.

4. Geoffrey Anketell Studder-Kennedy, *The Hardest Part* (Miami: Hardpress Publishing, n.d.), xiii-xv. Originally published in 1918. Emphasis is in the original.

5. Studdert-Kennedy, *Hardest Part*, 93–94.

6. Douglas, *Stand Your Ground*, 183–184.

7. Douglas, *Stand Your Ground*, 155.

8. Booty's exploration of the centrality of wholeness to our understanding of God can be found in *Reflections on the Theology of Richard Hooker*, 186–199.

Chapter 14: The Indissoluble Bond

1. The statement "love the sinner but hate the sin" does not appear in the Bible. A search of the entire Bible in the NRSV yields not a single instance in which "hate" and "sin" occur in the same verse. Search the King James version and you will only find one (Leviticus 19:17) which in no way means the popular epitaph. It is, in fact, the lead-in sentence to "love your neighbor as yourself."

2. Williams, *Where God Happens*, 83.

3. Douglas, *Stand Your Ground*, 176.

4. Vida Scudder, *Social Teachings of the Christian Year: Lectures Delivered at the Cambridge Conference, 1918,* ed. Christopher Poore and Andrew Raines (Galesburg, IL: Seminary Street Press, 2022), 140. Emphasis in the original.

5. Martin Luther King, Jr., *A Testament of Hope: The Essential Writings and Speeches of Martin Luther King, Jr.,* ed. James M. Washington (New York: HarperCollins, 1986), 577. The quote is from King's book, *Where Do We Go from Here: Chaos or Community?*

6. "House of Bishops, Pastoral Letter, November 9, 1933," in Armentrout and Slocum, *Documents of Witness,* 353, 354. Emphasis is mine.

Study Guide

1. "Resources," Kaleidoscope Institute, https://www.kscopeinstitute.org/free-resources. Accessed March 26, 2023.

2. Adapted from "Resources," Kaleidoscope Institute, https://www.kscopeinstitute.org/free-resources.

Selected Bibliography

Allchin, A. M. *Participation in God: A Forgotten Strand in Anglican Tradition.* London: Darton, Longman and Todd, 1988.

St. Ambrose. *De Nabuthae: A Commentary, with an Introduction and Translation.* Translated by Martin R.P. Maguire. Washington, D.C.: Catholic University of America, 1927.

Armentrout, Don S. and Robert Bloak Stocum, ed. *Documents of Witness: A History of the Episcopal Church 1782–1985.* New York: Church Publishing, 1994.

Athanasius. "On the Incarnation." In *Library of Christian Classics: Christology of the Later Fathers.* Translated by Archibald Robertson. Philadelphia: Westminster, 1954.

Augustine of Hippo. "Sermon 272." In Lawrence J. Johnson, *Worship in the Early Church: An Anthology of Historical Sources, volume 3.* Collegeville, MN: Liturgical Press, 2009, 76–77.

Baldwin, James. "The Fire Next Time." In *Baldwin: Collected Essays,* edited by Toni Morrison. New York: Library of America, 1998.

Boesak, Allan Aubrey and Curtiss Paul DeYoung. *Radical Reconciliation: Beyond Political Pietism and Christian Quietism.* Maryknoll, NY: Orbis, 2012.

Booty, John. *Reflections on the Theology of Richard Hooker.* Sewanee, TN: University of the South, 1998.

Brown Douglas, Kelly. *Stand Your Ground: Black Bodies and the Justice of God.* Maryknoll, NY: Orbis, 2015.

Brueggemann, Walter. *Interpretation and Obedience: From Faithful Reading to Faithful Living.* Minneapolis: Augsburg Fortress, 1991.

———. *Theology of the Old Testament: Testimony, Dispute, Advocacy.* Minneapolis: Augsburg Fortress, 1997.

———. *Reverberations of Faith: A Theological Handbook of Old Testament Themes.* Louisville: Westminster John Knox, 2002.

———. *Sabbath as Resistance: Saying NO to the Culture of Now.* Louisville: Westminster John Knox, 2014.

Countryman, L. William. *Good News of Jesus: Reintroducing the Gospel.* Valley Forge, PA: Trinity Press, 1993.

————. *Living on the Border of the Holy: Renewing the Priesthood of All.* Harrisburg, PA: Morehouse, 1999.

Day, Dorothy. *Loaves and Fishes.* Maryknoll, NY: Orbis, 1997.

————. "The Mystery of the Poor." In *Bread and Wine: Readings for Lent and Easter.* Maryknoll, NY: Orbis, 2005.

Dillard, Annie. *Teaching a Stone to Talk: Expeditions and Encounters.* New York: Harper & Row, 1982.

Dix, Gregory. *The Shape of the Liturgy.* London: Adam & Charles Black, 1945.

Dozier, Verna J. *The Dream of God: A Call to Return.* Boston: Cowley Publications, 1991.

————. *Confronted by God: The Essential Verna Dozier.* Edited by Cynthia L. Shattuck and Frederica Harris Thompsett. New York: Seabury, 2006.

Pope Francis. *Fratelli Tutti: On Fraternity and Social Friendship.* https://www.vatican.va/content/francesco/en/encyclicals/documents/papa-francesco_20201003_enciclica-fratelli-tutti.html.

Goza, Joel Edward. *America's Unholy Ghosts: The Racist Roots of Our Faith and Politics.* Eugene, OR: Cascade Books, 2019.

Hooker, Richard. "Sermon on the Nature of Pride." https://www.bartleby.com/209/179.html.

Irenaeus of Lyons. "Against Heresies." In *The Library of Christian Classics, vol. 1, the Early Church Fathers,* edited by Cyril C. Richardson, 358–368. Philadelphia: Westminster, 1953.

Johnson, Elizabeth A. *She Who Is: The Mystery of God in Feminist Theological Discourse.* New York: Crossroads, 1992.

Johnson, Lawrence J. "The Didache or The Teaching of the Twelve Apostles." In *Worship in the Early Church: An Anthology of Historical Sources,* 1:31–41. Collegeville, MN: Liturgical Press, 2009.

————. "Acts of Thomas." In *Worship in the Early Church: An Anthology of Historical Sources,* 1:240–243. Collegeville, MN: Liturgical Press, 2009.

Johnson, Luke Timothy. *Acts of the Apostles,* Sacra Pagina Series. Collegeville, MN: Liturgical Press, 1992.

Justin Martyr. *Writings of Justin Martyr.* Edited by Alexander Roberts and James Donaldson. Houston: Veritatis Splendor, 2014.

King, Martin Luther, Jr. "Where Do We Go from Here: Chaos or Community." In *A Testament of Hope: The Essential Writings and Speeches of*

Martin Luther King, Jr., edited by James M. Washington. San Francisco: HarperCollins, 1986.

Lichtenberger, Arthur. *The Day Is at Hand.* New York: Seabury, 1964.

Maurice, Frederick Denison. *The Kingdom of Christ.* Nashotah, WI: Nashotah House Reprint, 2013.

Merton, Thomas. *Spiritual Direction & Meditation.* Collegeville, MN: Liturgical Press, 1987.

Moltmann, Jürgen. *On Human Dignity: Political Theology and Ethics.* Translated by Douglas Meeks. Minneapolis: Fortress, 1994.

Nouwen, Henri. *Life of the Beloved: Spiritual Living in a Secular World.* New York: Crossroad, 1992.

Peterson, Eugene H. *Christ Plays in Ten Thousand Places: A Conversation in Spiritual Theology.* Grand Rapids, MI: Eerdmans, 2005.

Phillips, J. B. *Your God Is Too Small: A Guide for Believers and Skeptics.* New York: Simon & Schuster, 2004.

Potaro, Sam. *Crossing the Jordan: Meditations on Vocation.* Boston: Cowley Publications, 1999.

Richardson, Cyril C., ed. "The So-called Letter to Diognetus." In *The Library of Christian Classics, vol. 1, the Early Church Fathers.* Philadelphia: Westminster, 1953.

Rohr, Richard. *Everything Belongs: The Gift of Contemplative Prayer.* New York: Crossroad, 2003.

———. "Prayer as Political Activity." *Radical Grace (Newsletter of the Center for Action and Contemplation)* 2, no. 2 (March—April, 1989).

Schillebeeckx, Edward. *Christ: The Experience of Jesus as Lord.* Translated by John Bowden. New York: Crossroad, 1983.

———. *Jesus in our Western Culture: Mysticism, Ethics and Politics.* London: SCM Press, 1987.

———. *Church: The Human Story of God.* New York: Crossroad, 1990.

Scudder, Vida Dutton. *Social Teachings of the Christian Year: Lectures Delivered at the Cambridge Conference, 1918.* Edited by Christopher Poore and Andrew Raines. Galesburg, IL: Seminary Street Press, 2022.

Sedgwick, Timothy F. *Sacramental Ethics: Paschal Identity and the Christian Life.* Philadelphia: Fortress, 1987.

Selby, Peter. *A Public & a Private Faith.* Grand Rapids: Eerdmans, 1962.

———. *Instead of Death.* New York: Seabury, 1963.

———. *Free in Obedience.* New York, Seabury, 1964.

————. *BeLonging: Challenge to a Tribal Church.* London: SPCK, 1991.

————. *Dissenter in a Great Society: A Christian View of America in Crisis.* (Eugene, OR: Wipf & Stock, 2005.

Studdert-Kennedy, Geoffrey Anketell. *The Hardest Part.* Miami: Hardpress Publishing, n.d.

Temple, William. *Christianity & Social Order.* London: Shepheard-Walwyn, 1976.

Thurman, Howard. *Jesus and the Disinherited.* Boston: Beacon Press, 1976.

Turner, Philip. *Christian Socialism: The Promise of an Almost Forgotten Tradition.* Eugene, OR: Wipf & Stock, 2021.

Tutu, Desmond Mpilo. *No Future Without Forgiveness.* New York: Image Books, 2000.

Underhill, Evelyn. *The Spiritual Life: Four Broadcast Talks.* Mansfield, CT: Martino Publishing, 2013.

Waddell, Patrick. *Charles Gore: Radical Anglican.* Norwich, UK: Canterbury Press, 2014.

Weil, Louis. *Sacraments & Liturgy: The Outward Signs.* Oxford, UK: Basil Blackwell, 1983.

Williams, Rowan. *Where God Happens: Discovering Christ in One Another.* Boston: Shambala Publications, 2005.

————. *The Way of St. Benedict.* London: Bloomsbury Continuum, 2020.

Wink, Walter. *Engaging the Powers: Discernment and Resistance in a World of Domination.* Minneapolis: Fortress, 1992.

Winner, Lauren F. *The Dangers of Christian Practice: On Wayward Gifts, Characteristic Damage, and Sin.* New Haven: Yale University, 2018.

About the Author

Michael W. Hopkins is a priest of The Episcopal Church. Ordained in 1990, he has served congregations in Washington, DC; Glenn Dale, Maryland; and Rochester, New York. He currently lives in Hornell, New York with his spouse of 31 years, John Clinton Bradley. He holds an M.Div. from Seabury-Western Theological Seminary and an MFA from Seattle Pacific University. He was a student in the doctoral program in theology and liturgy at the Catholic University of America for three years. He was also President of Integrity, the advocacy and fellowship organization for LGBTQ+ Episcopalians and their supporters from 1998–2003. He currently sits on the boards of CASA-Trinity, a regional addiction services provider, and the Finger Lakes SPCA.

Printed in the USA
CPSIA information can be obtained
at www.ICGtesting.com
JSHW050349120823
46425JS00002B/3

9 781640 656505